HEARING
THE HEARTBEAT OF
GOD

MICHAEL NEELLEY

 THE PEOPLE'S SEMINARY PRESS

HEARING THE HEARTBEAT OF GOD

The People's Seminary Press
P.O. BOX 410
Burlington, WA 98233
www.peoplesseminary.org

ISBN – 978-1-954387-10-2
E-Book ISBN 978-1-954387-11-9

Made in the U.S.A.

Cover art used by permission from the Pilgrim Center of Hope (https://pilgrimcenterofhope.org/)

ENDORSEMENTS

There's been a growing sense for quite a while that the wineskins that hold our conceptions of faith and church and God are cracking yet it's unclear what the alternatives are. Mike speaks to the hunger and thirst many of us have felt for a long time and shows not a new program, plan, or formula but, as a weathered guide, invites us on a journey of hope where we will find ourselves in one way or another. Mike engages the holistic complexity of humanity while clearly exuding a confidence of one who has tasted and seen that there is indeed more. He does us a service not by providing simple solutions or quick answers but through the courage to name the vulnerability that many of us feel but are afraid or unable to admit as well as the path forward that we may have all but given up on.

This is a journey rooted in the kindness of God in places and ways we've been longing for, in the very places and ways we may have all but given up on. The journey is also an invitation to a partnership with God and the power of the Spirit that can help us see that more is possible, and that more is going on, than the tiny, sanitized boxes of modernity would have us believe. I've seen it, I've tasted it, and I've been brought to tears witnessing the Kingdom come in ways I dreamed about in seminary but wasn't sure was possible.

—Jon Epps
Bellingham, Washington

The anonymous author of *The Cloud of Unknowing* taught that "nobody's mind is powerful enough to grasp who God is. We can only know him by experiencing his love." Mike Neelley has given us here a glimpse into the mysterious, transformative experience of God's love. He explores both Scriptural and experiential depths to convey these truths that he has learned at the feet of Jesus. Mike approaches the heart of Jesus with consuming wonder and rapt attention. As with all truth he can only narrate what he has discovered, and it is up to us to experience our own journey into the great mystery. But his words are a true and good guide, a North Star in the night sky that affirms: "Jesus loves us and wants to share his heart with us." With our eyes fixed on this, we will not go too far wrong.

—Aaron White
Author of *Recovering: From Brokenness and*
Addiction to Blessedness and Community

For the last 35 years as colleagues together in pastoral ministry Mike has shared, with humility and transparency, his own journey of intimacy with God in ways that encourage and challenge my own willingness to allow the Holy Spirit deeper access to my heart. This book offers others this same privilege of spiritual companionship with Mike on the journey to accept Jesus' invitation to encounter God's heart.

—**Rev. Dr. Laurie Brenner**
Senior Pastor
West Side Presbyterian Church

In *Hearing the Heartbeat of God,* Mike Neelley has given us a vital roadmap into the journey of deeper intimacy with the Trinity. Through the transparent sharing of his own journey he welcomes us to join him in a deep and abiding love affair with Creator God. Providing us fresh understanding of others who have walked this journey before us, Mike gently compels us to listen to the voice of the Holy Spirit and dive deeper into the heart of our God.

Mike provides clarity and detail for our healing journey that helps us understand God's lavish grace and unfailing love. We are provided with insights of pitfalls and ways to not be trapped by our own life pain. We are invited to look deep into our life experience to understand ourselves through the lens of being God's beloved child. We are provided guidance in walking alongside others in this journey of transformation and an invitation to partner with the Trinity in the healing of our communities. Mike's invitation is accompanied with clear ways to apply what he is teaching us. Each chapter has a spiritual practice to deepen our understanding and actually experience the truth he is offering.

This is a book I will read and reread, allowing its truths to become part of the fabric of my life. I urge you to dwell deeply here and to allow the Holy Spirit to show you through Mike's words the joy of a deep, abiding love affair with our Triune God.

—**Rev. Rita Nussli**, MSW
Spiritual Director, SoulFormation

This is an important book for all those seeking a deeper and more abiding life in God. Throughout the chapters Mike brings us a deeply personal yet communal journey asking what it means to truly be forgiven and enter into a living relationship with Jesus. By opening his heart and soul to us, Mike offers that rarest of things: a very real and profoundly compelling reason to experience all that God calls us to. I encourage you to make space for this beautiful book not only on your bedside, but in your heart as well.

—**Jeff Keuss**
PhD Professor of Theology
Seattle Pacific University and author of
Live the Questions: How Searching Shapes Our Convictions and Commitments (IVP)

I've been waiting eagerly to read this book – and I was not disappointed! Mike has delivered an inspiring and enlightening guide to going deeper into the heart of the trinitarian God. He expands our understanding of the fatherhood of God, introduces us to a dynamic relationship with Jesus the Son, and reinstates the Trinity's missing person – the empowering Holy Spirit.

Mike exemplifies speaking truth in love, writing with both honesty and humility. He is not the hero of all his stories. He is sensitive to the pitfalls and obstacles of overemphasizing some truths at the expense of others. He shows us that hearing God's heartbeat is intensely personal, but also has implications for our relationships and social context.

Over the last few years, I've been privileged to journey with Mike enough to know that he is a reflective practitioner — doing what he says while analyzing and evaluating deeply at the same time. I'm happy to give my endorsement and recommend this book to all who desire to go deeper into the heart of God.

—**Paul S. Olver**, D. Min.
Pastor and Spiritual Director
President, Impact Latin America
Seattle, Washington

Mike offers an extraordinary gift in these pages...the story of his journey deeper into God's love. Mike's story involves fear, shame and protective walls, things familiar to many of us. But his story is also thick with the healing presence of Jesus, present in the midst of it all, tenderly, persistently, lovingly inviting him to open all the rooms of his 'heart home' to God's healing love. Mike shares deeply from his personal experience, rich with encounters with Jesus in imaginal prayer and prophetic promptings from the Holy Spirit and significantly formed by years serving with Tierra Nueva in the jails and recovery halls of northwest Washington. He weaves his own story with Scripture reflection and engagement with a wide variety of spiritual mentors including Brad Jerzak, David Benner, Ruth Haley Barton, Bob Ekblad, and more.

As a Reformed Christian who tends to get stuck in her head, *Hearing the Heartbeat of God,* was a gift. Mike's Presbyterian background combined with his deep engagement with Scripture and thoughtful interaction with a wide variety of Christian authors provided the solid foundation I needed to feel comfortable descending into my own heart home with Jesus. The Activations at the end of each chapter provide wonderful opportunities to step into a wide variety of prayer practices, some familiar, some stretchingly new.

As I set down *Hearing the Heartbeat of God,* I find myself yearning for more...more of Jesus, more of the Holy Spirit, more of my heart and life given over to God. I can't think of a better reason to endorse a book!

—Rev. Summer Mohrlang
Executive Director, SoulFormation

TABLE OF CONTENTS

ACKNOWLEDGEMENTS

As I discover more of God's goodness in Jesus through the Holy Spirit, it has been vital for me to learn to hear, discern, and follow God's voice. This living interaction with Jesus is the breath of life in my relationship with God. If I could pass this learning on to others, I would be doing what I was created to do. I am also grateful for the many people who have passed this learning on to me over the years.

I am deeply indebted to the mentoring and teaching of Brad Jersak, especially his book, *Can You Hear Me? Tuning in to the God Who Speaks*, which has been foundational for my understanding and practice of hearing God. I have given his book away to more people than I can remember. As I sensed the Holy Spirit inviting me to write on this topic, I realized that Brad's teaching has become so deeply ingrained in my thinking and practice that it is hard for me to know where his thoughts end and mine begin or differ. Sometimes I will share ideas that I first heard from him, and yet the way that God has interacted with me through them is unique to me. I talked with Brad about this, and he graciously said, "Just say that. Go for it!"

I have also been profoundly shaped by and grateful for the ministry and mentorship of Bob & Gracie Ekblad and other staff at Tierra Nueva, the international Christian nonprofit the Ekblads founded, which seeks to share the good news of God's total liberation, healing, and transformation in Jesus with people from the margins of society, especially those affected by immigration, incarceration, and addiction. The stream of God's work at Tierra Nueva is what Bob calls "Word, Spirit, Street." This unique expression of church in North America combines an emphasis on social justice issues, Scripture, and the empowerment of the Holy Spirit for inner healing and transformation, physical healing, deliverance from spiritual bondage, and hearing God's voice. While this book is the fruit of over forty years of my life with Jesus, the thirteen and a half years I worked at Tierra Nueva have dramatically shaped that relationship.

I also want to acknowledge with gratitude the teaching, experiences and encouragement I've received through Presbyterian Reformed Ministries International (PRMI). Since my introduction to this stream of the Holy Spirit in 2002, I have grown in my involvement with PRMI as participant, intercessor, prayer team member, worship leader and teacher. The PRMI Dunamis conferences have been fertile ground for my encounters with God's heart.

Thank you to my wife, Susan, who continually encouraged me to make room for this project and celebrated my small victories along the way. This book would not have come into being without you as my partner.

Thank you to the long list of dear friends who read my biweekly updates and keep me covered with prayer. Thanks to Cari Armbruster, Heidi Basley, Libby Chapman, Kitsy Gregory, Eric Stelter, James Kearny, Cathy Owens, Scott Sund, Jennie Spohr, Jeff Keuss, Tom Johnston, Jon Epps, and Matt McCoy for reading my drafts, giving me feedback, and praying through this book with me.

And an enormous debt of gratitude to my editor, Karen Hollenbeck Wuest, who took this rough wooden spoon, polished it, and helped make it beautiful.

FOREWORD

"If you love me, obey my commandments. And I will ask the Father, and he will give you another Advocate, who will never leave you. He is the Holy Spirit, who leads into all truth. The world cannot receive him, because it isn't looking for him and doesn't recognize him. But you know him, because he lives with you now and later will be in you. No, I will not abandon you as orphans—I will come to you. Soon the world will no longer see me, but you will see me. Since I live, you also will live. When I am raised to life again, you will know that I am in my Father, and you are in me, and I am in you. Those who accept my commandments and obey them are the ones who love me. And because they love me, my Father will love them. And I will love them and reveal myself to each of them."

Judas (not Judas Iscariot, but the other disciple with that name) said to him, "Lord, why are you going to reveal yourself only to us and not to the world at large?"

Jesus replied, "All who love me will do what I say. My Father will love them, and we will come and make our home with each of them."

—John 14:15–23 (NLT)

Michael Neelley has afforded me the great honor of framing his book with a foreword about the most beautiful mystery I know: the reality of God—Father, Son, and Holy Spirit— making a home *within us* to reveal the infinite, intimate love of the triune God. Mike rightly refers to that home as a "heart house," and I've indulged in citing Jesus' "last will and testament" from John 14 at length, because it explicitly locates the Spirit (v. 17), the Son (v. 20), and the Father (v. 23) *within each of us.* Individually and collectively, our hearts are the "house of God"—the temple where the living Lord has chosen to make himself at home . . . forever!

Christ's beautiful words at "the last supper" (as recorded in John 13–17) confirm Paul's testimony to the Corinthians, which is that the God who lives in each of us is *not* some "speechless idol" (1 Cor 12:2), but is loving, caring, forgiving, personal, and responsive. When we call on this personal God, we can expect an answer (Jer 33:3). On that fateful night of "the last supper," the verbs for divine communication tumble out of Jesus: the Spirit *will never leave us* (v. 16); *will lead us in truth* (v. 17); we *know him*, and he *lives with us* (v. 17); we are *in him* and he is *in us* (v. 20). By the Spirit, Christ will continue to reveal himself to us, teach us, guide us, counsel us, advocate for us, testify to us—through both our spiritual ears (hearing) and eyes (seeing).

Since God's thoughts about each of us outnumber the sands on the seashore (Jer 33:22), we should be far more surprised when God seems silent than when God is talkative! After all, Pentecost is the celebration of a Spirit who *gushes* (not *trickles*) revelation to *all* flesh—people of every age, sex, color, and social standing. And what the Spirit reveals is the *good news* of Jesus *in each of us!*

As Mike demonstrates from Scripture, from his experience in ministry, and from his own journey, the river of God flows from a spring at the very core and center of our being: our heart house. Mike is a long-term practitioner and facilitator of "listening prayer," and he has applied those gifts in pastoral, prophetic, inner healing, and community justice ministries. I can testify firsthand to the healthy practices that generated this book. Mike is also adept at helping those who have difficulty journeying into their heart house or hearing from God, and so if you run into obstacles along the way, you've found the right teacher!

Some of us might stumble over Jesus' words in John, when he says, "*If* you love me." Does this suggest that his promises are conditional? Weren't the conditions fully met by Christ himself in his passion, resurrection, ascension, and on Pentecost? Of course they were! And so how can we understand these "*if* you love me" statements?

I suggest that the *truth* of the covenant becomes the *experience* of its promises in us as *Love* opens our individual eyes, ears, and hearts to say *yes* to that unconditional river of love flowing through our lives. John himself said, "We love *because* he first loved us" (1 John 4:19). In loving God *in response to* the love he *first* showed to us, our hearts are softened, our ears are opened, and our eyes are cleansed so that we can *experience* the living voice of Christ more clearly.

I encourage you to be accompanied by Mike Neelley as he invites you to listen to God in your own heart house. Because Mike loves Jesus wholeheartedly, he will inspire you to love Jesus as well. Though the prophetic world (like every world shaped by human culture) has become corrupted by egos and agendas, we do not need to become cynical about the personal prophetic or threatened by prophetic justice in the Bible, for Mike's simple and sincere devotion to Jesus can bring us back to God's heart of love for *all* people. I commend his gentle wisdom to you without reservation or hesitation. Enjoy!

Bradley Jersak
The Feast of the Ascension, 2022

INTRODUCTION

The central truth and conviction of this book is that Jesus loves us and wants to share what is on his heart with us.

When I talk about *hearing* God, I am referring to the day-to-day lived reality of our relationship with God. I am not talking about random signals we receive from a disconnected voice or an impersonal spiritual power source or something only mystical Christians can do, but a conversation with *someone* who actively loves us, whose name is Jesus. Jesus brings us to the heart of the Father[1] and gives us his Spirit so that we can experience the Father's longings for us.

When we expect God to speak and anticipate that we can hear from God, we enter into a place of abiding love and intimacy within the heart of God. We are also invited into a life-giving journey of co-laboring with the Holy Spirit.

I have often heard faith described as "belief with expectation attached to it," and I used that phrase a lot until Brad Jersak, the author of *Can You Hear Me? Tuning in to the God Who Speaks,* suggested that I replace the word "expectation" with "expectancy." He explained that "expectation" can have negative connotations about how we *expect* God to answer specific prayers. If those prayers aren't answered, we can become disappointed, disillusioned, or even resentful. "Expectancy, on the other hand, is genuine trust that God will move (even powerfully) but the word is focused on my openness, welcome, and gratitude to God specifically, as a good Father with good gifts, without demanding a particular outcome (even though I'm free to make specific requests)."[2]

We often believe all sorts of things about God or intellectually agree with certain theological statements. Yet, to use Brad's term, our beliefs don't necessarily lead us into the realm of vibrant *expectancy* about our relationship with God.

My friend Drew points out that the invitation to "taste and see" that God is good is not an invitation to "think and agree," but to *experience* God. If we don't ever taste, see, or experience God, it can be difficult to live with expectancy. If we don't live with expectancy (or faith), we aren't looking for God or anticipating that God will move, and so we may miss out on what God is already doing right in front of us. The good news is that God is the initiator: "This is love, not that we loved God but that He loved us and sent His Son" (1 John 4:10). Ultimately, it isn't up to us, for God pursues us, speaks to us, and reaches out to us *first*—before we ever do anything.

For twenty-one long years, I struggled as I believed in Jesus and hoped for heaven, continually trying to be good through my own efforts—a dry obedience with no sense of God's tangible goodness or presence. I often felt like I was stumbling in the dark. But after experiencing some inner healing and spiritual liberation from bondage and false beliefs about God and myself, I began to have an expectancy (and experience) that God would share his heart with me in my daily life. I looked forward to it! I loved Jesus and couldn't wait to be with him. After this dramatic shift, I began to encounter God's goodness as I joyfully sought to be near the one who was already coming near to me.

Shortly after I entered this season of new joy and freedom in drawing close to Jesus, I was asked to be in charge of the prayer ministry at my church, and then I was invited to preach on prayer. I dove into books on prayer and began to write my sermon, but one morning, after writing in a coffee shop, I realized that I had been reading and writing about prayer, but I hadn't really prayed. As I sat in my car, I prayed, "Jesus, what do you want to say to your people?" Immediately, I heard, "Tell them I love them and want to spend time with them."

Jesus offers *each* of us this invitation to come into his presence and to spend time with one who loves us and calls us "beloved."

Hearing God's voice is an adventurous journey into the heart of God, who loves us. Along the way, we will be humbled by God's grace and goodness in speaking to us and inviting us into all that he is doing. We will also be challenged as God highlights the parts of us that are resisting his invitation and not trusting his love. We may also find ourselves frustrated when we can't hear clearly or when there are the long stretches of silence. And we may be disappointed when we do not hear the responses we want.

As we embark on this journey, I want to reflect on the icon that is on the cover of this book, which depicts a scene from the Last Supper, where the Gospel of John describes the "disciple whom Jesus loved" as "reclining" against Jesus' "bosom" (13:23). In this intimate scene, the beloved disciple not only hears what Jesus is saying, but he also feels Jesus' heartbeat. This same word is used earlier in John to describe the intimate relationship of the Son to the Father as being "in the bosom of the Father" (1:18). This is the invitation, and it will take us deeper than we imagine.

Shortly after St. Augustine's conversion, he prayed, "O God, let me know myself; let me know You," for he was convinced that the discovery of God was connected to the discovery of the self—and that the discovery of the self was connected to the discovery of God.

As we seek to hear the heartbeat of God, we will come to know God more intimately, which will lead us to know the truth of ourselves more intimately as well. On this journey, we will discover a deeper sense of both our brokenness and our belovedness.

This book is rooted in my own experience of deepening intimacy with God, and so is part memoir and part teaching. It is not so much "how to" as "come and see." It is full of stories about my encounters with God and my experiences of hearing the heart of God as well as my obstacles and filters and what God has taught me in those places. My hope is that these stories and questions will encourage you to deepen your expectancy about encountering God.

As you read, you may find yourself thinking, "I'm not like that. God doesn't talk to me. I could never have encounters with God like that." But rather than reading my stories from a place of comparison, I invite you to let them guide you towards new possibilities and new ways of experiencing God.

Throughout the book, I encourage you to keep returning to the opening invitation of this book: *Jesus loves us and wants to spend time with us so that we can intimately know God's heart and hear God's voice.*

May our hearts and imaginations be open and expectant to hear Jesus' invitation to encounter the heart of God so that we can trust his goodness and love for us more deeply. May we live with vibrant expectancy as we discover that God delights in us, loves us lavishly and without conditions, and wants to share his heart with us.

I encourage you to take your time on this journey. God is not in a rush. The prayer activations at the end of each chapter create space for you to *activate* what you have read. This journey is not about getting more correct information about God, but encountering the goodness of God in the living Jesus so that we can abide with God's heart and connect with what is happening in our own hearts.

> *I pray that the Father of glory, the God of our Lord Jesus Christ, would impart to you the riches of the Spirit of wisdom and the Spirit of revelation to know him through your deepening intimacy with him. I pray that the light of God will illuminate the eyes of your imagination, flooding you with light, until you experience the full revelation of the hope of his calling—that is, the wealth of God's glorious inheritances that he finds in us, his holy ones! I pray that you will continually experience the immeasurable greatness of God's power made available to you through faith. Then your lives will be an advertisement of this immense power as it works through you!*
>
> –Ephesians 1:17–19 (*The Passion Translation*)

I pray that as we journey deeper into the heart of God, we will have living encounters with Jesus and hear the heartbeat of God's boundless love for us as we seek to perceive God's deepest longings for our lives.

PART I:

INWARD

Chapter 1

HEART HOUSE

. . . that according to the riches of His glory [the Father] may grant you to be strengthened with power through His Spirit in your inner being, so that Christ may dwell in your hearts through faith . . .

–Ephesians 3:16–17

When I was in my late forties, I began to wrestle with known and unknown fears, along with anxiety, defensiveness, and unhealthy ways of protecting myself. Over time, these struggles began to cause what my wife described as "soul-crushing stress." I felt stuck in my relationship with God and others, and I didn't like myself, and so I began to seek counseling along with healing prayer.[3]

One rainy December afternoon, I made a two-hour drive to meet with a friend for tea and prayerful conversation.

After talking for a while about the many places I felt stuck, we entered into prayer, and she asked the Holy Spirit to guide me into a particular place where I might be stuck. I found myself returning to a memory from my teenage years that carried a lot of shame and darkness, a time when I despised myself for what had happened and felt powerless for allowing it to happen.

We invited Jesus into this memory and asked him to show me his presence and love. I had an impression of him standing in a corner of the room, and as we continued in prayer, I sensed Jesus kneeling down and shaping something with his hands. In my imagination, I went over to the corner and saw a small structure on the floor. His hands were wrapped around it, and it looked like he was building a wall around it.

"What is that?" I asked

"It's your heart," he said.

I silently wondered why he was building a wall around my heart, but as we continued praying and listening, I felt a strong yearning to ask Jesus to restore all that had been stolen from me through my shame-filled memory. As I spoke this prayer, I wept for all I'd lost and felt a deep assurance that Jesus would answer my prayer for restoration.

Sitting with one hand over my heart and one on my head as I prayed with my eyes closed, I saw myself walking on a wide gravel driveway. On my left was a dark and dingy two-story house on a large property. On my right, a tall hedge wrapped around the spacious yard. The house felt like a beach house, though I couldn't see the ocean. Stairs led from the gravel driveway up to a wide front porch to the house, which was all closed up, with all the window shades pulled down.

I became conscious that I was both participating in and observing this vision. As I stood in the driveway staring at the house, I kept asking, "What is this? Why am I seeing this?"

Then I heard, "This is your heart."

As I described this vision to my friend, I wondered how this dark, dingy, closed-up house was somehow a representation of my heart.

Over the next months, I periodically sought out this vision in prayer and kept seeing myself standing in front of that house that was somehow my heart, but I never felt stirred to go inside.

Selah[5]

About six months later, I met to pray with another friend about some other places that felt stuck in my relationship with God. As prayed through the walls that had surfaced, my friend led me to pray:

> Holy Spirit, I want to make room, so that all the places in me that have been self-sufficient would now be God-sufficient. They are open to you. Thank you for wanting to comfort, nurture, and teach me. I want to know you in those ways. I invite you to expand your influence in me, increase your effect on me, and take

up all the room you want in me. I don't want to be self-sufficient.
I don't want to self-protect.

I welcome you to move in. Open all the doors to any places that
have been shut up or locked way. Every place where I've been
happy with what I've had, show me what more looks like. Take
my hand, welcome in! All my windows are open, filled with light.

As I prayed with my friend, I suddenly found myself back in my
vision, but I was no longer standing in the driveway—I was inside my
heart house!

I had not told my friend about the heart house vision I'd had a half-
year earlier and how my heart had been closed up until that very moment,
but I found myself praying, "Thank you, Holy Spirit for waiting for me
to be willing to invite you in. Thank you for the amazing heart you have
given me, for wanting to move in, for opening all the doors and windows,
for helping me take all the dust covers off the furniture. Now is the time
for you and me to explore this house."

As the Holy Spirit led me through my heart house, I looked around at
the dark wood trim and box-beam ceilings. In the dining area, I noticed a
long window seat looking out on the yard. In the second-floor bedroom,
I felt moved to ask the Holy Spirit to help me remodel the room, which
felt small and plain. One wall came down, creating a sitting area with
huge picture windows, two chairs, and a small table. From the second-
story window, I could see over the hedge surrounding the house and was
delighted to see sand dunes rolling down to an expansive beach and then
the ocean. My heart was a beach house that God had designed and deco-
rated *with* me!

I prayed, "Thank You, Father, for my heart house, which is so beautiful and restful. Thank You, Holy Spirit, for this place to meet with you
that has such a beautiful view."

As I described all that I was seeing to my friend, she remarked that
the ocean might represent God's vast love and the sand on the beach
could reflect the number of God's thoughts toward me (Ps 139:17–18).
She invited me to ask God to reveal those precious thoughts to me over
the days and weeks ahead.

"Some days, you might say, 'Father, what room do you want to visit today?' And when he takes you to a new space, you could ask, 'Why are we here? What is it about this room that you want to show me?'"

Later that evening, I sat in my office at home, and I recorded this prayer encounter in my journal. When I came to this invitation from my friend, I stopped and asked the Father what room he wanted to visit. Immediately, I found myself in the basement of my heart house, which was set up as a workshop with various machines. I did not recognize most of the machines, but some were very large and new and seemed to have one specific function, while others looked like antiques that were in excellent condition. Though I didn't know how to use these machines, I sensed they were all for the building projects that I was going to do with the Father. In this space within me, I already had what I needed to create and build with my Father!

Struck by the creative function of each machine, I prayed, "Father, will you teach me how to use these tools? I don't know how."

"Of course," God said, "my son, Jesus, is a carpenter."

"Is there a particular work you want to show me?" I asked.

In the corner, I saw a workbench with a small vise mounted on it, similar to one my dad had in his workspace in our garage when I was young. Clamped in the vise, I could see a long, thin piece of wood, which was carved like a miniature canoe.

"What is this?" I asked.

As I looked, the canoe became a Viking ship with a dragon-shaped bow, several large sails, and numerous oars running along each side.

I sensed that the simple canoe was something I could build on my own, but the beautiful boat that God was building was powered by the wind of his Spirit along with a community of many rowers.

CONCLUSION

My journey into my heart house has helped me to encounter the living Jesus in my own heart, where I regularly meet with God to hear and discern something of his heart and purposes for me. These meetings have become part of "the immeasurable riches of God's grace in kindness toward [me] in Christ Jesus" (Eph 2:7).

At the end of each chapter, I will offer a question or prayer exercise to help you connect with what you are reading. I encourage you to engage each of these activities before moving on to the next chapter. I also encourage you not to compare your experiences with mine or anyone else's. Simply let the stories help *activate* your sense of expectancy for encountering God.

ACTIVATION

In John 14:23, Jesus says, "If anyone obeys my teaching, my Father will love them, and We will come and make our home with them." The Father and Son desire to make a home in *your* heart through the Spirit. Take some time now to make space in your heart to connect with your desire to spend time with God. Then connect with God's desire to spend time with *you*.

Relax and be still. Take a few slow, deep breaths, centering yourself on the truth that God is right here with you, right now. He has never left you, and he has made a home within your heart. Pause and take a moment to thank God for making a home within you.

Now invite God to lead you into the meeting place of your heart.

As you enter this space, you might keep repeating a simple phrase, such as, *Jesus, I welcome you in my heart.*

After settling into this space, take a moment to pay attention to what it looks like. Do you notice any unusual or distinctive features? Now ask Jesus to guide you on a tour through this space.[6]

Throughout the next week, keep returning to this space and anticipate meeting God there. Record images and insights from these meetings with God in your journal.

Chapter 2

INVITATION TO INTIMACY

Abide in Me, and I in you. As the branch cannot bear fruit by itself,
unless it abides in the vine, neither can you, unless you abide in Me.
I am the Vine; you are the branches. Whoever abides in Me and I in
them, [they are] the ones who bear much fruit, for apart from Me
you can do nothing.

–John 15:4–5

Several years ago, I was in the Downtown Eastside neighborhood of Vancouver, British Columbia with Tierra Nueva's certification program for Transformational Ministry on the Margins,[7] which seeks to train ministry workers in marginalized contexts. My role was to pray with people and help lead the worship,[8] but then Bob Ekblad, Tierra Nueva's founder and senior leader, asked me to teach a section on "the Father heart" of God.

As I waited for the session that I would be teaching, Bob's wife, Gracie, shared about her complicated relationship with her dad, which stirred me to reflect on how I'd been critical of and hurt by my dad for years because he had not pursued a relationship with me. I had always been the one to initiate a call or write a letter. If I wanted a relationship with my dad, I had to pursue him, and I had often resented this. But as I listened to Gracie, I realized that for a long time, I had also felt as if I had been the one pursuing in my relationship with God. Though I knew this wasn't theologically true, I had been relating to God through the filter of my negative experiences with—and judgment of—my earthly father. While the concept of relating to God through my parental filter was not new to me, this specific realization about feeling like the pursuer in the relationship was altogether new.

Later that night, as I was falling asleep, I suddenly realized that I needed to forgive my dad for not pursuing me and then release him from my judgments against him. This kind of forgiveness work is a regular part of the prayer ministry of Tierra Nueva.[9] As I lay in bed, I named how I felt wronged by my dad and then I forgave him and handed him over to Jesus. Then I confessed and repented of relating to God through this same filter, speaking out that God, the father of Jesus, is not like my earthly father, for his love always pursues me first, *before* I have done anything to seek him. I ended by telling God that I was looking forward to the extravagant ways that he would reveal how he was pursuing me in love.

Over the subsequent weeks, as I anticipated these extravagant changes in how I experienced God's pursuit of me, I began to recognize that my pursuit of God wasn't actually as earnest as I had imagined it to be.

That winter, as we prepared to enter the new year, my wife, Susan, suggested that we take some time to reflect on the previous year and dream about the year ahead. As I thought about this, I realized that I couldn't remember much about my journey from the previous year. I looked through my journal for clues about where I'd been and what I'd done over the previous twelve months. Through the fog of my memory, I began to see a path—much like a high alpine trail above the tree line, marked by rock cairns whenever the path isn't clear. Every six to eight weeks, I found a journal entry reflecting on the invitation from John 15:4–5 to abide in Jesus.

I also noticed that following these reflections on the invitation to abide, I would confess and apologize for *not* abiding. As I prayed about this, I recognized that God had been calling me to *abide* in him, but I had been busying my days with "spiritual" work and professional ministry. Though I was praying and reading Scripture in preparation for certain tasks, I was not nurturing a relationship with Jesus. I kept apologizing to God for my distance, for not lingering in his presence, and for not being still before him. I wanted God's help in my work and life, but I wasn't connecting with God's heart—or my own heart. My time with Jesus often seemed utilitarian rather than intimate.

The next morning, as I prayed, I found myself returning to the porch of my heart house, and I noticed an addition on the south side of the house. As I walked around the porch to the right, I came to two French doors, which opened into a library or study. I squinted through the windows, but I couldn't see God the Father. As I looked behind me, I saw two Adirondack chairs in the distance, situated on the crest of the sand dunes, alongside a small table with two cups of steaming coffee. My Father was waiting for me in one of the chairs.

I walked through the coastal morning air that was both salty and damp, cool and warm at the same time, then sat in the chair next to my Father as the early light emerged behind us, illuminating the foam on the waves. In silence, we gazed at the horizon beyond the surf, and God gestured toward the vast waters. Immediately, I thought of the ocean as an image of the breadth, length, and depth of God's love.

In my thoughts, I heard God say,

"Mike, you love to describe the ocean of my love to people. You observe it, study it, and sing about it, but you haven't ventured very far into it yourself. You walk on the beach, listening to the crashing roar. You wade in up to your knees, sometimes even your waist, but how can you really *know* the depth of my great love if you don't go beyond the waves close to shore?"

I knew God was right, but I didn't know *how* to venture away from the safety of the shore, deeper into the ocean of his love.

"You have no idea how wide and deep my love for you is," God continued. "You still think it is full of conditions, that you have to perform. But my love is unfathomable."

I longed to encounter this unfathomable love, but I felt powerless to make that happen.

In the following weeks, I prayerfully tried to imagine myself out in the middle of the ocean, far from land, where I couldn't see the shore. Or I tried to dive deep under the water, but I kept bobbing to the surface. So I tried to imagine myself wearing scuba gear, plunging deep into the darkness of the vast sea of God's love, but my imagination would flail, and I would find myself safely out of the water, back on the shore.

Finally, I gave up and prayed, "Father, I can't explore the depths of your love on my own. You are going to have to take me there."

MAKING OURSELVES AVAILABLE TO GOD

In *Sacred Rhythms*, Ruth Haley Barton writes about her experience of exhaustion in ministry from constantly seeking to measure up. In response to her crisis she writes, "Am I willing to rearrange my life for what my heart most wants?"[10] As I reflected on these words shortly after giving up and inviting God to take me to the depths, my own weariness and longing were awakened. Her words challenged me to express my "willingness to God directly, acknowledging the mystery of spiritual transformation and *[my] powerlessness to bring it about.*"[11] (emphasis added) These words invited me into a new freedom, helping me perceive that "spiritual transformation at this level is a pure gift as we make ourselves available to God."[12]

Slowly, over the next months, I began to "rearrange my life," intentionally setting aside time to give God my undivided attention. Though I sometimes felt overwhelmed about how or where to start, Barton helped me clear away the clutter by inviting me to practice "breath prayer" as "an expression of [my] heart's deepest yearning coupled with the name for God that [was] most meaningful and intimate for [me] at [that] time."[13] I began to get up earlier so that I could spend twenty minutes being still and present to God, breathing in and out prayerfully. As I practiced abiding in Christ,[14] my breath prayer became, *Father, take me deeper in Your love.*

I would breathe in, *Father.*

Then breathe out, *take me deeper in your love.*

I knew that I needed to free this prayer space from any expectation that God would *do* anything, *say* anything, *solve* anything, or *show up* in any tangible way. I needed to let go of transactional expectations and simply hold a space of being still and knowing that God is God,[15] receiving whatever the Father wanted to give me by faith, whether or not I was aware of any tangible *experience*.

Over time, abiding with God like this became a regular practice, where I didn't seek to accomplish or produce anything by my own effort. I wasn't trying to perform through my devotional practices so that God would "show up" and help manage my life circumstances. I wasn't seeking to create a spiritual experience or check the prayer box of my religious accomplishments.

As I sat in that silent space, I was often distracted and sometimes fell asleep. But as I kept breathing in, "Father," and breathing out, "take me deeper in your love," I sensed my heart paying more attention to God's heart. Every once in a while, something would bubble up out of the depths that seemed to be from God's heart, either for me or for someone else. From time to time, the Holy Spirit would drop a person's name on my heart whom I hadn't been thinking about.

The first time this happened, I was out for a short hike after twenty minutes of silent prayer, rejoicing in the day, and the name of a friend came to me as a small and subtle whisper. Perhaps my time of silent prayer had made me more sensitive to hearing this name in my thoughts, a tender shoot springing from prepared soil. I hadn't had any interaction with this friend for some time, and so I assumed this prompt was from the Holy Spirit, so I prayed, "Father, her deeper in your love." After this prayer, I felt stirred to pray specifically for her work situation.

When I returned from my hike, I sent her an email to tell her that God had put her on my mind. She quickly responded, "One of my prayers this morning was that God would remind me of His love for me and that I matter to Him. Your email is most definitely an answer to that prayer." She went on to describe some struggles she was having in her work.

This sort of *name dropping* has become a regular way that God is communicating with me and pursuing me, the fruit of soil prepared by my time of abiding with him. The Holy Spirit has also brought to my mind places where I need to do deeper work of repentance in myself or extend forgiveness toward others. These interactions with God have been so encouraging and life-giving.

After an extended season of praying, "Father, take me deeper in Your love," I felt drawn to return to my heart house, and Jesus led me to a door in the center of the main floor that I hadn't seen before. Jesus opened the door, and I peered down a long, steep stairwell that I presumed led to the basement. Together, we started down the stairs, which led down and down, further and further. We didn't talk, but just kept descending. I noticed that the walls and stairs were carved out of stone, and the space was well-lit, though I couldn't see any noticeable source of light.

Because I was with Jesus, I trusted that he was leading me on this never-ending stairwell, and so I didn't feel worried or claustrophobic. Eventually, I felt released to step out of this imaginative praying, even though we had not yet finished the descent or reached any destination.

Over the next several weeks, I periodically returned to my heart house in prayer and found myself with Jesus, still descending that long stairwell.

Finally, one spring morning, we reached the bottom of the stone stairs, which opened into a large, round stone chamber. The ceiling was about fifteen feet above us and inset into the walls of the chamber I could see a dozen or more colored doors. I stared at the doors, wondering where they might lead, as Jesus stood beside me. Neither of us moved.

Over the few next weeks, every time I returned to my heart house in prayer, I found myself standing with Jesus in the middle of this stone chamber, staring at these colored doors. Then one day, I found myself stepping forward, and one of the doors opened, and I sensed Jesus saying, "This is the room called *Pretend*."

Immediately, I thought, *This is the room where I store all the masks and personalities I wear so that people will like me and I will be accepted. This is the room where I hide all the ways I've learned to act and present myself to others.* I knew that this room reflected who I had pretended to be, all the personalities I'd projected for so long that I could no longer distinguish my pretend self from my authentic self, the self that is created in the image of God.

I saw the personalities I had tried on as an adolescent so that I would be accepted and liked by my friends. I saw the parts of myself I had hidden from my friends, because I was afraid that I wouldn't belong.

I saw the parts of myself that had experienced rejection tucked away to be kept from further embarrassment.

I saw my college roommate's friend, who could recite all the funniest lines by the comedian Steve Martin, mimicking his tone and mannerisms. I remembered how we had laughed until we cried and how I had wanted to be funny like this guy so that I could make people laugh.

As I remembered this guy who was trying to be like Steve Martin, I thought, "How far will I go from my true self? I was trying to be like a guy who was trying to be like another guy!"

I also saw the times I had pretended to agree with people just to avoid conflict so that I wouldn't feel rejected or shut down. I saw all the ways I had tried to pretend to be good, when really I knew that my heart was full of judgment, resentment, pride, superiority, passive aggression, apathy, lust, fear, and anger. I had locked all these things away, because I was afraid these things would prove that I was not a good person.

As I realized that all of these memories were crammed into boxes that were stacked on top of each other, weighing down shelves that were overflowing with years and years of hoarded, accumulated garbage, I moaned, "Jesus, this room is overwhelming. What do I do with all this stuff?"

I felt exposed and uncomfortable and found it difficult to breathe. I wanted to do something and felt anxious to get busy and to start cleaning up this room so that I could make myself more presentable before God.

But then, by the grace of God, I stopped and said,

"Jesus." I took a deep breath, filling my lungs. Then I exhaled and prayed, "As you take me deeper into your love, will you sit with me in this overwhelming space?"

Selah

Later that afternoon, I read *The Gift of Being Yourself* by the Christian psychologist, David Benner, which illuminates the relationship between the journey of self-discovery and knowing God. The following passage, in particular, lit up the page:

"The self that God persistently loves is not my prettied up *pretend* self but my actual self—the real me. But master of delusion that I am, I have trouble penetrating my web of deceptions and knowing this real me. I continually confuse it with some ideal self I wish I were."[16]

As the word, "pretend," reverberated through me again, I sensed the invitation to "be still and know that I AM God."[17]

After being still for several minutes, I returned to Benner, who writes, "Real knowing of ourselves can only occur after we are convinced that we are deeply loved precisely as we are."[18]

I sensed a deep awareness within my spirit, a longing to know the deep and wide love of God for *me*— the *real* me, not the one I had imagined for myself, or pretended to be, or projected for everyone else to see. I cried out for God to awaken in me both the depth of my brokenness and the depth of my belovedness.

Deep in that subterranean chamber in the room called "pretend," I realized that for months, I'd been praying, "Father, take me deeper in your love," and this prayer had brought me into a room filled with all my unfixed garbage, which is precisely where God wanted to reveal the depths of his love for me. All my other experiences of God's love had been near the surface, observing from the shore, walking in the shallow water, playing in the waves, and I had assumed that I had done something to deserve them. Yet my journey to this room had brought me far beyond the waves into the deep water of God's unmerited, undeserved love. At the bottom of the long stairwell in my heart house, stripped of all my masks, I discovered that even my true self was truly beloved.

DEEPER IN HIS LOVE

My journey with Jesus hasn't always been in that place of a deeper knowing of my true self or wanting Jesus to sit with me there. Many years prior to this imaginative prayer experience, I had gone to see a new spiritual director,[19] and he asked me about my journey with God. I had been learning a lot about the power of the Holy Spirit in bringing healing and deliverance, and so I shared about areas where I was seeking healing and deliverance.

Then my spiritual director asked a question that unsettled me: "What if you asked Jesus to come sit with you in your mess? What would that be like?"

I didn't like this suggestion. I didn't want Jesus to sit with me—I wanted him to fix me! While real healing is part of the kingdom of God, and deliverance can release us from places where we feel stuck in our relationship with God and others, we often need to engage in long, deep, slow work around the habits and ways of thinking that led us into our stuck places in the first place.

Not long after that meeting with my spiritual director, I was reading an Advent devotional that included the gospel passage of Peter's three denials of Jesus from Luke 22. At the moment of the third denial, the rooster crows, and Jesus turns and looks at Peter across the courtyard. The writer of the devotional comments, "At that moment Peter was fully known and fully loved." And then Peter weeps bitterly.

As I read these words, I felt the presence of God come into the room where I was sitting, a huge invisible presence that pressed in upon me. It felt as if God was inhabiting every single atom of the room, and the atmosphere felt heavy, as if I were at the bottom of the sea, and there was absolutely no place where I could hide. I felt utterly exposed, full of shame and failure, and I didn't want God to come near me, but the presence continued to fill the room, and I continued to feel the terrible discomfort of God's holy, totally *other*, yet non-judgmental presence amidst my not-cleaned-up, not-fixed, not-healed, not-delivered self where I was fully known and fully loved.

As I reflected on this uncomfortable experience, I read a reflection by Thomas Ashbrook in his book on the writings of St. Teresa of Avila: "He loves the real you, not the person you wish you were. If you look for His love there you will miss it. We can't really know God's love for us until we know the one He loves."[20]

I realized with discomfort that my desire for intimacy with God was actually very shallow. I wanted to feel close with God, which I had thought would fill me with a sweetness and goodness that would comfort, encourage, and build me up. Instead, I had felt naked and uncomfortable, a raw intimacy I've heard described as "into-me-you-see." In this place, I sensed God saying, "I am here with you. I see it all and I am staying right here with you."

David Benner helps frame these raw, vulnerable encounters with God by noting, "A complete knowing of our self in relation to God includes knowing three things: our self as deeply *loved*, our self as deeply *sinful*, and our self as in a process of being *redeemed* and *restored*."[21] (emphasis added)

Now in the deep stone chamber of my heart house, in the room called "Pretend," Jesus came to sit with me. Rather than being shocked or judgmental, Jesus didn't ask me to clean up my mess, and he didn't clean up my mess for me either. Nor did he leave me because he was too holy to look upon it all. Instead, he sat with me, and we waited together, just as we had waited at the bottom of the stairs. Way down in my subterranean room of pretend selves, I knew myself as deeply *sinful*. With Jesus beside me, I also knew myself as deeply *loved* and could begin to believe that I was in the process of being *redeemed* and *restored*. In becoming more aware of what is truly in my heart and then welcoming Jesus into these hidden areas of shame, I trust that I am very slowly being transformed into the image of Jesus.

Our journey deeper into hearing the heartbeat of God is also a journey deeper into our own hearts, so that we can come to know that we are fully loved right in the midst of our most shameful, hidden, and unhealed places, in spite of all our untransformed strategies and failures. As Paul puts it, "God showed His love for us in this, *while we were still sinners* Christ died for us; while *we were weak*, while *we were enemies*."[22] (emphasis added) The good news that Jesus brings is not that God will love us once we get our act all cleaned up and all our bad stuff fixed, managed, or hidden away.

Rather, the good news is that the Father immeasurably loves us as we *really* are—our deeply flawed, sinful, weak, broken, enemy selves—and so he sent his Son to the depths of hell—which includes our personal hells— to rescue us from the powers of darkness and bring us into the kingdom of the Beloved, where we can become our *true* selves.

CONCLUSION

I think it is important to begin our journey with these reflections, because our end goal is not simply to hear God's voice so that God will answer our questions or prayers or encourage our faith. Rather, we are seeking to hear God and know God's heart so that his love will transform us. Our journey into hearing the heartbeat of God is about the communication that happens when we experience an authentic and vulnerable love relationship with God so that "[we] shall know fully even as [we are] fully known."[23]

If going deeper into the heart of God and your own heart feels daunting, be encouraged by Ruth Haley Barton, who says, "The decision to give ourselves to the experience of [hearing God] brings us to the very edge of what we know and leaves us peering into the unknown."[24] Yet how can we know what we can't know? How can we do what we don't know how to do?

Barton points out that the "the stirring of spiritual desire indicates that *God's Spirit is already at work within us*, drawing us to himself... We reach for God because God first reached for us. Nothing in the spiritual life originates with us."[25] (emphasis added) The desire to connect more deeply with God is *already* being stirred in us by the Holy Spirit so that we can begin to hear God's voice and know God's heart.

While I have focused on my brokenness in this invitation into intimacy, it is important to know that going deeper in the Father's love isn't only about revealing the depths of our brokenness so that we can know God's love in those places. On this journey, we will also discover the beautiful, powerful, and mysterious parts of ourselves that have been buried deep within those hidden places. These things may seem too good to be true, but this is where we will find our calling. "For we are God's work of art, created in Christ Jesus for good works that we would find our life and joy in doing them" (Eph 2:10). God has put beautiful things in us to live out, and we may have buried some of them deep within the hidden stone recesses of our heart.

ACTIVATION

Breath Prayer

Set aside ten or twenty minutes. Then find a place that feels comfortable and safe, where you will not be overly distracted and can make space for God. Sit quietly for a few moments. Take several deep breaths through your nose, exhaling through your mouth. Pay attention to your breathing and what you are feeling in your body. If you feel tension, put a hand on the place where you feel it. Breathe in God's peace. Release anxiety as you breathe out. Spend a little time paying attention to breathing and what you are feeling in your body.

> You might use the breath prayer, *Father, take me deeper in your love.* Or you might create a breath prayer of your own.
>
> Breathe in, *Father,* or *Abba.*
>
> Breathe out, *take me deeper in your love.*

In this space, release your desire to make anything happen during this time. Invite God to be with you. Acknowledge your desire to hold space to devote your attention to God. Consent to God's presence within you and around you.

When you notice yourself dwelling on a past event, return to your breath prayer. As you begin to think about future stresses, return to your breath prayer. When you become distracted by thoughts of the day, return to your breath prayer. "If your mind gets distracted 1,000 times in 10 minutes of silent prayer, it's 1,000 opportunities to come back to the loving presence of Jesus."[26] Be kind to yourself as you seek to *return* your attention to the loving embrace of God. *Returning* is a habit that will take time to build.

After five or ten minutes, spend some time writing about your experience. Let your writing emerge as a conversation with Jesus.

Chapter 3

The Journey into God's Heart

"Grant, Lord, that I may know myself that I may know Thee."

–St. Augustine, *Confessions*

While God communicates with us at various points in our journeys—often before we are even aware that such a journey has begun—the invitation to journey into God's heart beckons us to draw closer to Jesus. As noted in the introduction, we see this intimacy in John's description of the Last Supper, where he says that "the disciple whom Jesus loved" is "reclining in the bosom of Jesus."[27] In other words, he has his head on Jesus' chest. This image suggests that the disciple is not only listening to Jesus' *words*, but also to Jesus' *heart*. When we attend to God's heart, we will need to draw close to Jesus and seek deeper intimacy with Jesus, for he is the one who will reveal the Father's heart to us.

You may have assumed that reading this book would give you some tips and tools so that you could hear God better. You may have thought hearing God's voice is like tapping into a power source, something that we can use at will to serve our religious purposes, or to validate us in some way. Yet this journey into hearing God's heart is really about nurturing an intimate relationship with Jesus and surrendering to God's purposes so that our hearts can listen for God's still, small voice. The theologian and devotional writer A.W Tozer describes how God longs to be in relationship with us, writing that "God is a person, and in the deep of His mighty nature He thinks, wills, enjoys, feels, loves, desires and suffers as any other person may."[28] So our invitation is not just to listen for God's *voice*, but to draw close to God's *heart*. As John writes in his Gospel, "This is eternal life, *that they might know You*, the only true God and Jesus Christ whom You have sent."[29] (emphasis added)

God is always seeking to communicate with us, at every stage of our journey. Even before we knew God or set out to follow the path of Jesus, God was inviting us into a relationship of love—not so that we could know more information *about* God, but so that we could experience an intimate relationship *with* God. In Paul's letter to the Ephesians, he prays to "the Father of glory, that we would have a spirit of wisdom and revelation in the knowing of Him."[30] Later, Paul prays that we would "know the love of Christ that is beyond knowing."[31] We can only know something that is beyond our capacity to know if it is *revealed* to us. God created us to be in a relationship with him so that we could *know* God and God could *reveal* his love to us.

This knowing is foundational and fundamental to our Christian maturity. Such knowing is not about acquiring more information about God or knowing and keeping all the rules for religious and moral behavior, nor is it about knowing the "right" theology. While these things are part of God's revelation through time and history, the invitation to each of us is to grow in an intimate, experiential knowing of God, the Father of glory, so that our hearts and lives will be transformed into the likeness of Jesus,[32] his beloved son, who is close to the Father's heart.[33]

As we come to know God's heart more deeply, God will also reveal more about our own hearts.

As noted in the introduction, St. Augustine and many others talk about the necessity of this twofold revelation. The psychologist David Benner observes that "neither can proceed very far without the other. Paradoxically, we come to know God best not by looking at God exclusively, but by looking at God and then looking at ourselves—then looking at God, and then looking at ourselves. . . . Both God and self are most fully known in relationship to each other."[34]

This journey into discovering the goodness of the heart of God, along with our own brokenness and belovedness, will lead us to wrestle with the painful discovery that everything within us is not transformed the moment we ask Jesus into our lives. In fact, the very presence of Jesus within us will challenge and provoke all the things in us that are not aligned with his heart.

But the journey always begins with God's loving pursuit of us. We can only love because God loved us first. We can only pursue God because he pursued us first. God is always pursuing us, even in the midst of our sin and brokenness. In the next sections, I describe some of my early journey toward God's heart, my own brokenness *after* encountering Jesus, and my experience of God's ongoing pursuit, which has led me into deeper freedom and deeper knowledge of myself as well as the love of God.

MY EARLY JOURNEY: FALLING INTO— AND OUT OF—GOD'S GRACE

I spent my first twenty-one years as a Christian believing that I was a disappointment to God, which seems strange since the gospel is meant to be *good news*.

When first I entered this new and strange relationship with Jesus at the age of fifteen, my parents had recently divorced. I had been raised in the Catholic Church but had left that behind a few years before. The chaos of adolescence raged around me and within me. Though I couldn't articulate this at the time, I desperately wanted to belong somewhere, to fit in, to know I was accepted. I was full of confusion and felt utterly lost.

My introduction to how I could have a relationship with God only added to my confusion. Over a two-year period, a handful of Christian classmates kept inviting me to their church and various church events, telling me that I needed to ask Jesus into my life so I could have a personal relationship with him. As a former Catholic, this concept was new to me, but I found these conversations intriguing, and so I went to their meetings, but resisted their pressure to "invite Jesus into my life."

Much of the popular theology during this time in the 1970s focused on the "end times" or "last days." This eschatological teaching was popularized by Hal Lindsay's books, *Late, Great Planet Earth* and *Satan is Alive and Well on Planet Earth*, along with Christian apocalyptic movies, such as *A Thief in the Night* and *A Distant Thunder*, which depict the final days of planet earth, when God's enemy, the Antichrist, will rise up and persecute Christians for seven years and God will pour His bowls of wrath out on the earth to punish the devil and those who don't believe in Jesus. The message I received was that God was getting ready to punish us, and Jesus was coming back any day to take the faithful ones with him to Heaven, and whoever was left behind was going to suffer under the reign of the Antichrist.

Though the popular Christian story still proclaimed that God loved us, and that Jesus had died for us so that we could be in *right* relationship with God, the message focused on how we would be *saved* from the Antichrist *and* from God's wrath by putting our faith in Jesus and asking him to forgive us and come into our hearts. After listening to this message for two years, I eventually wanted to make sure that I was on the right side when the "end times" wrath hit the fan.

In retrospect, I can see that my new faith seemed a lot like taking out a fire insurance policy to ensure that I would not suffer the red-hot wrath of God, which was going to be pouring over the earth any day. Yet this anger was couched in the language of God's saving love. Thus the message I took away was that Jesus' love and forgiveness would save me from the anger of God, the Father. Though I now consider this theology to be deeply troubling, these friends helped open my eyes to the possibility of having a *relationship* with God.

As my Christian classmates pressured me for those two years to become a Christian, I remember telling them that Christianity kind of seemed like a drag, a bunch of do's and don'ts. While I didn't really know what the "do's" might be, I was pretty sure that the long list of "don'ts" included a lot of the things I was doing. I also that knew it would cost me to change, and I wasn't sure I was ready to pay the price.

Then one day, my friends gave me a religious tract, "The Four Spiritual Laws," and the prayer at the back said, "If you truly desire Jesus to be Lord of your life, pray this prayer and He will come into your life as He promised."[35]

I already felt like I didn't belong at home or school, and I was pretty sure that if I said "yes" to Jesus, I would be unmoored from every last thing that offered stability in the chaos of my young life. Then I had the thought that if God was real, he could take care of my fears. And if God *wasn't* real, then nothing would really change if I prayed this prayer. So, why not give it a shot and see what happens? I prayed and asked Jesus to "sit on the throne" of my life, as the tract suggested. As I stood in the middle of the street near my high school, praying this prayer, I looked up and it seemed as if everything around me brightened and came into focus, like the sun coming out from behind a cloud. I also realized that I was grinning from ear to ear.

In the days that followed, I became aware of the presence of God pursuing me. I wasn't looking for God, but I started to notice his presence everywhere, which was both unsettling and exhilarating.

A few weeks after asking Jesus to make his home in my heart, I was on the Oregon coast for the weekend with my mom and sisters. As I wandered around the beach town with the son of the family we were staying with, I had a strong, uncomfortable feeling that something was both following me and was also *in* me. I sensed this presence, strange and other, in a place that had been previously empty. While the presence didn't seem dark, it unnerved me. Though I had asked Jesus to come make his home "in my inner being by the Holy Spirit,"[36] I hadn't understood how this would *feel*.

Over the next weeks, I sensed this Presence often, and I came to understand that God was not only strangely within me, but also around me in my room at night when I attempted to pray. I would sit on my bed and talk out loud, and God seemed to be with me, communicating back to me. This gave me an inexplicable sense of security and comfort amidst of the chaos of my life. When I tried to describe these nighttime conversations to my classmates, they seemed to think I was as strange as I already felt.

While I sensed Jesus pursuing me, I didn't change many of my previous habits, even though I knew that they were probably on God's "don't" list.

A year or so later, I was smoking pot with a friend one night in the back parking lot of a church that was situated at the end of a backstreet in our small town, surrounded by trees, with no regular traffic, and no one at the church on weeknights. As we smoked in his car, I started to feel convicted that it was wrong for me to use marijuana.

While sitting on my friend's car door, leaning against the roof, looking up at the night sky, I prayed, "If this is wrong, God, give me a sign."

I waited. There was nothing, not even a shooting star.

"I didn't think so," I thought.

Then I dropped my eyes from the starry expanse and found myself looking across the top of the car at a red and white stop sign. S. T. O. P.

I'd asked for a sign, and so I dropped the joint.

Though this may seem like a funny coincidence, I have since returned to this spot several times, and there is *not* a stop sign in the parking lot. There never has been. It's just a gravel lot behind a little, small-town church, and there is not a stop sign visible anywhere down either street. Whether God put a sign there, or I was so high that I imagined it, God used that sign to communicate that he was pursuing me and wanted me to trust him.

After I graduated from high school and went to college, this communication with God seemed to dry up. Though I became involved in a college group at a large Presbyterian church and ate up the teaching about God and loved the sense of belonging with my Christian friends, we did not engage in conversation about how God might communicate with us in real time or in real ways. It seemed that God could only communicate with us through the Bible and the church. Because there was so little anticipation about how we might experience God's tangible presence in our day-to-day life, my faith seemed to be up to me and my own efforts to live a moral life based on biblical values.

Over time, I slipped back into my default way of thinking about Christianity as a religious list of do's and don'ts. If I could just keep Jesus happy by following all the rules, I'd stay on the "right" side of God's anger when the judgment day came. These rules were based on the Bible as well as the spoken and unspoken religious rules of my church culture.

Though I clung to the hope that I was "saved" and forgiven and would be in heaven someday, I found myself increasingly afraid of standing before the throne of God's judgment in heaven. As I imagined a giant screen broadcasting my sins to all who were watching, God's unconditional love began to feel like a "bait and switch." Though I had been saved *from* sin and forgiven *for* my sin as a gift of God's unconditional grace, my ongoing relationship with Jesus seemed to be about trying hard not to sin and to be good through *my own* efforts. Yet I felt completely powerless to change anything about myself. I read my Bible a lot, went to church regularly, prayed every day, and did all sorts of religious stuff to check the boxes and be a good Christian in the eyes of God and the church community. But deep down inside, I felt a tremendous guilt for my failures, along with fear, condemnation, and futility.

This drove me to become increasingly depressed, as I felt stuck in a sin-confess-sin-confess shame cycle. My Christianity had not brought me freedom, for I only experienced moments of fleeting joy when I thought I was doing "well." Stories of mature Christians walking in victory only made me feel a greater sense of failure. I practiced what one of my friends called *sin management*, where I walled off areas of my life hoping they would not overflow or get out of hand. I measured myself harshly in certain areas of life while neglecting many others. And I was sure that God was just as disappointed in me as I was in myself. While I said that I loved God and he loved me, I didn't *want* to come close to God, because I was afraid of what he might ask of me if I truly surrendered myself to him.

I was sure that if I drew close to God, he would only confirm the condemnation that I so regularly heaped on myself. So I hung around Jesus in public, but I avoided coming close to God in private. Though I prayed because praying was part of being a good Christian, the thought of actually coming close to God in prayer became terrifying. My prayers were like driving up to a fast-food drive through—I would place my order and then go on my way, without coming close to God or sticking around to sit down and enjoy the banquet feast. I was most certainly never resting my head against Jesus' chest!

Because religion was both my lifeline and a harsh taskmaster, as I judged myself, I became full of judgment toward others. Judgment became a kind of addiction for me, a way of comforting myself and recovering a sense of power in my powerless spiritual life. If I could judge someone else, I'd feel better about myself for a little while. I'd judge people for their sinful actions, though I was often guilty of the same things. And I'd judge people for not reading their Bibles, or not going to church, or not being involved in the religious gatherings where I was involved. I wouldn't speak these judgments to others, but I judged people within my heart. As Jesus said of the Pharisees, I was like "a white-washed tomb, looking clean on the outside but full of dead men's bones."[37]

During this time, I also became involved in full-time church youth ministry, and I eventually went to seminary so that I could become a pastor. I was trying to teach youth and adults about Jesus, but as Rob Reimer says in his book on inner healing, *Soul Care*, "You teach what you know but you reproduce who you are."[38] So I was talking about a relationship of love with Jesus but emphasizing behavior and belief. Thus I was reproducing all the same religious baggage that I was living—trying hard to be good, to do the "right" religious things, and to believe the "right" theology.

This focus on right behavior and right belief summed up the Pharisee's heart within me. Thus my belief in Jesus wasn't *good news*, but had become a toxic form of religion for me and for those I was teaching. When our faith is measured by belief and behavior, we are not living in the freedom and joy of an intimate relationship with Christ but have turned to an empty religion that has nothing to do with the grace of Christ.

The apostle Paul criticizes this strongly in his letter to the Galatians:

> I am astonished that you are so quickly deserting him who called you in the grace of Christ and are turning to a different gospel . . . Mark my words! I, Paul, tell you that if you let yourselves to be circumcised, Christ will be of no benefit to you. You are severed from Christ, you who would be justified by the law; you have fallen away from grace".[39]

The phrase, "fallen from grace," is often used to describe someone who has *fallen* from a prominent position into immorality. Yet Paul is not talking about immorality in this passage, but religious legalism. When we measure ourselves or others by a set of prescribed rules, we *fall* from the freedom of God's grace through Jesus into a legalistic, performance-based religion that ceases to be *good news* to the world.

I had definitely fallen from the grace of my early encounters with the presence of God in upper rooms and parking lots. This trajectory of legalism and my ongoing struggles with sin brought me to the edge. I had become a depressed, conflicted Christian. While I proclaimed the unconditional love of God to those around me, I was not experiencing that goodness or unconditionality myself. Yet somehow, I couldn't throw it all out. So I cried out like Peter after many disciples had stopped following Jesus, "Lord, to whom shall we go? You have the words of eternal life, and we have believed and have come to know, that you are the Holy One of God."[40]

MY LATER JOURNEY: ENCOUNTERING THE *GOOD NEWS* OF GOD'S BOUNDLESS FREEDOM AND LOVE

About twenty years after I first committed my life to Jesus, when I was in my mid-thirties, I led a youth mission trip on the Crow Indian Reservation in eastern Montana. One afternoon, as I wandered through the sanctuary of the church where we were staying, I found a handout in the pulpit that talked about "spiritual strongholds." As I read the pamphlet, several headings seemed to be highlighted for me: fear, sexual sin, and control.

I breathed deeply and prayed, "Okay, God. I trust that you are showing me these things. Please help me do something about them."

Over the following weeks, these areas seemed to become a battleground rather than a place of victorious conquest. Filled with a deep sense of futility about my ongoing failure, I sank deeper into despair.

Then a friend suggested that I read Neil Anderson's *The Bondage Breaker: Overcoming Negative Thoughts, Irrational Feelings and Habitual Sins."*

As I read the words in the subtitle, I thought, *Check. Check. Check.*

This book helped me to recognize many of my unhealthy beliefs about God and the false ways I'd come to feel accepted, significant, and secure. It taught me that my new identity in Christ was based solely on the work of Jesus—and that has nothing to do with what I do or don't do, have done or have not done. Though I might have heard these things in the past, by the grace of Jesus, I could now receive them. Behind my self-condemnation in the battleground of my mind, I began to hear the true voice of Christ, who has complete authority over the devil, our flesh, and the world. Like a surgeon, this book cut me open. Through ongoing prayer, it removed the cancerous growths that had grown in my heart and mind. I devoured its good news like a starving man.

When Anderson spoke of "taking every thought captive in obedience to Christ,"[41] I was painfully aware that I had never taken a thought captive a single day in my life. To the contrary, I was captive to my thoughts. My mind was like an open field, receiving whatever seeds fell there, which seemed to be mostly negative weeds.

In the Parable of the Sower,[42] Jesus describes a farmer liberally sowing seed in all kinds of soil—a hard-packed path, where birds quickly come to snatch up the seed; on rocky ground, where it grows quickly but doesn't last because it has no root; on neglected ground, where weeds grow up and choke the plant so that it cannot bear fruit; and on good soil that is carefully tended, where it produces a huge crop.

As I read *The Bondage Breaker* and prayed through the prayers at the back of the book, God began to pull out the weeds that had grown up over my heart and mind so that the good plants that were already growing in me could finally flourish and begin to bear fruit. It wasn't about me trying to clean myself up so that God would plant good things in me or finally decide I was good enough to pour down his love upon me. Rather, through prayer, I entered a partnership with the Holy Spirit so that God could begin to remove obstacles that were keeping me from experiencing the love that God had *always* been pouring over me.

This truly *good news* gave me a completely new mindset.

As I entered this new season of my life with God, I found myself falling in love with Jesus and experiencing his goodness. Rather than being afraid of God and filled with self-condemnation, I couldn't wait to be with him. I was free from the fear that God was disappointed in me, and I was no longer afraid of what God might say to me. My prayer life was no longer like a fast-food drive through, where I put my order in and then quickly drove off, hungrily devouring things that wouldn't truly nourish me in the privacy of my own car. Instead, I began reclining at the banquet table with my Beloved, putting my head on his chest, and listening to his heart as I digested the nourishing and beautiful things he prepared for me. After stumbling in the dark for twenty-one years, afraid to come close to the heart of God, I entered a living conversation with Jesus, and this relationship has become light and life to me.

CONCLUSION

I have shared the first half of my journey with God in this chapter in order to highlight how we often come to our relationship with God with "weed" seeds of brokenness and confusion already sown into our hearts. These weeds don't automatically disappear when we come to Jesus, and they continue to determine how we perceive ourselves and our broken-ness, and our ability to receive our belovedness. These weeds must be pulled out by their roots so we can hear God and receive what God is saying to us about his purposes for our life.

While hearing God's heart can be as simple as knowing that Jesus is our Good Shepherd, and as his sheep we can recognize his voice, we also need to learn to discern what is coming from Jesus and the heart of God—and what is coming from our experiences of wounding and brokenness, and other voices. Part of that discernment is about learning to listen to our own hearts and seeking to co-labor with the deep work of the Holy Spirit so that we can experience more of the freedom and wholeness that God intends for us as his beloved children.

Jesus continues to take me deeper into hidden places within my own heart so that I can discover the parts of me that haven't been fully restored to God's goodness and mercy. Some of the foundational theologies that have formed my faith still need to be deconstructed or reframed. This journey continues as the Father draws me deeper into his love.

ACTIVATION

Before beginning the activation, find a place where you can make space for God. Sit quietly, taking several deep breaths through your nose and exhaling through your mouth. Then take a few minutes and center your attention on our breath prayer. *Father, take me deeper in your love.*

As you rest in this space of being *beloved*, invite the Holy Spirit to bring to your mind something that you have believed that stands in opposition to the love that God wants to communicate to you.

Wait quietly, returning to your breath prayer, as this fear, wound, disappointment, or false belief rises within you. As you breathe, hold this before the loving heart of God.

As you continue to breathe, *Father, take me deeper in your love,* invite God to reveal how this disappointment, false belief, fear, or wound has colored what you believe about God and how God feels about you.

As you continue to breathe, invite God to guide you in responding.

Take a few moments to record anything that God has revealed to you in your journal.

Conclude by inviting the Spirit to reveal a truth from Scripture that can counter this false belief, wound, disappointment, or fear.

Chapter 4

HEART THEOLOGY

"Mother is the name of god on the hearts and lips of all children."

—Alex Proyas, *The Crow*

In the 1994 movie *The Crow*, the protagonist (Eric Draven) confronts the heroin-addicted mother of a young girl he has befriended. As the Crow (Draven) stands behind the mother in the bathroom, pushing heroin out of her arm, he makes her look at herself in the mirror and then says, "Mother is the name of god on the lips and hearts of all children."[43]

Our beliefs about God inform how we relate to God and how we *think* God relates to us, and what we think is on God's heart for us. These beliefs are most powerfully shaped by the messages and experiences we received from our parents or caregivers, as they were the primary nurturers and authority figures in our early lives. In *The Deeply Formed Life*, pastor Rich Villodas calls these messages, "scripts," which he describes as "the messages we receive, the roles we are given, and the ways we believe we must live that have been consciously handed to us or subconsciously interpreted by us."[44]

These scripts often remain buried deep within us, and yet they inform what I describe in this chapter as our *heart theology*. In *Evangelizing the Depths*, Simone Pacot, frames such theology and the internal journey toward healing and intimacy with God in terms of evangelism, noting that there are some parts of ourselves that still need to be won over to the goodness of God. She writes, "The question is whether the good news of Christ's message of life has reached into our deepest impulses, the most deeply buried and acute difficulties, our death wishes, our instincts of destruction and self-destruction."[45]

With all that is going on inside us and shaping our thinking, we may wonder *how* we can possibly ever know that we are hearing from the heart of God?

Though my relationship with my mom has also shaped my heart theology, throughout this chapter I am emphasizing the way that my relationship with my dad colored my perception of God's relational involvement in my life. Obviously, our heart theology is impacted by our mothers and fathers, and so it is important to unearth the messages and experiences we have received from both our parents.

An example of this comes from *SOZO* (the Greek word for "saved, healed, delivered"), an inner healing ministry at Bethel Church in Redding, California that seeks to get to the root of things that hinder our relationship with the Father, Son, and Holy Spirit. This ministry often equates the dynamic of our relationship with God the Father to our relationships with our fathers, and our relationship with the Holy Spirit to our relationships with our mothers.

What is "Heart Theology"?

When we first come to faith in Jesus, we are often responding to an invitation that is framed by a theological understanding of *who* Jesus is (e.g. "the author and finisher of our faith" [Heb 12:2]), what he has *done* (e.g. he died for our sins on the cross), and what he is *like* (e.g. the Good Shepherd [John 10:11] or the Way, the Truth, and the Life [John 14:6]). It makes sense that Jesus is the Way into this relationship.

We take this new framework of beliefs about Jesus, (and the Father, and the Holy Spirit depending on our theological tradition), and we transpose them over the internalized and largely unconscious messages we received from our parents.

These new beliefs may be about the good news of the love of Jesus, or God's faithfulness, or how God is trustworthy and will never leave us. All these things are good, true, and beautiful, and we may be in strong intellectual agreement with them, but our *heart theology* shapes what we believe deep down about our intimate relationship with God—how we interact with the Father and how we believe God relates to us. On the surface we are receiving and believing new information, while our hearts are still driving the bus. As Simone Pacot urges, we need "to become aware of the disconnect between what we say we believe and what we really believe at core. Right here, for many of us, there is a real spiritual struggle."[46]

We see this struggle with the people of God in the book of Exodus. Through Moses, God rescues the Israelites from four hundred years of enslavement in Egypt with "a mighty hand and an outstretched arm." Once the people are free, God invites them to follow him in the wilderness, but rather than drawing close to God, the people are afraid and ask Moses to serve as their go-between. Though their bodies are free and they are no longer living in the land of their oppression or under the system of forced labor, they are bound by a generational mindset that was formed over centuries through the people's experiences of trauma and oppressive authority. Thus they see Moses as a taskmaster and slave driver, inflicting the will of God, and they understand God as the cruel, punishing Pharaoh. Because the *heart theology* of the Israelites continues to be shaped by the long story of oppression and trauma in Egypt, a whole generation cannot enter the Land of Promise, and they never enter the fullness of their relationship with God.

Similarly, as we seek to hear God's heart for us, we might be living out of our early relationships with our earthly fathers and mothers or other authority figures. Though we might be able to talk, sing, and teach about the love of God, many cannot experience that love because our hearts are bound by old narratives and cannot receive this good, new story. Our heart theology functions as an unconscious operating system deep within us, shaping how we relate to God. This system needs to be healed and liberated before we can enter into the fullness of God's promise and hope for our lives.

But if we want to get in touch with our heart theology, we must first be willing to face the dynamics that we grew up with in our family systems.

When I was young, I often felt my dad's anger simmering beneath the surface, like a dormant volcano that I was always afraid would erupt one day. I sensed a fearful power, and so I drew back. I don't think my dad wanted me to be afraid of him, but I was afraid of disappointing him and experiencing his displeasure. He was never physically or verbally abusive, but the anger I sensed within him or which he expressed often controlled the atmosphere of my childhood. Sometimes, he was tender, and other times he was hard to please. Sometimes he shamed me, and others he affirmed me. As I got older, I often felt confused and pressured by our nightly ritual, where I was expected to give him and my mom hugs and say, "I love you," because my experience of "love" seemed to be conditional and connected to my performance that day.

Because I didn't feel safe disagreeing with him or having a different opinion, my strategy was to remain silent and acquiesce. Once, as an adult, he complained that none of his children ever shared anything of consequence with him. In a bold moment, I asked if he wanted to know the reason. "Yes," he said. I told him that when anything we valued conflicted with his values, he shut the conversation down. I held my breath, and after a pause, he admitted, "You're right. I do that."

Another strategy I had was to try to keep enough of the rules to be the good son in order to avoid his disappointment. But as I distanced myself in hurtful ways and my failure to live up to his expectations brought about the very thing I'd been trying to avoid, for when I was twenty-five, he wrote me a letter listing all the ways I'd hurt him or let him down. The list was accurate and included the pain I'd caused him in my not visiting him while he was being treated for cancer. He concluded the letter by saying, "I will go on with my life without a son and you go on without a father."

This concluding sentence pretty much sums up the heart theology I inherited from my family system.

Although I came to faith in Jesus hearing about the unconditional love of God, my heart related to God through rules and conditions that I didn't keep very well. I tried to relate to God through my performance, always trying to be good enough, but I also kept my distance and never felt safe to come close. I *believed* in God, but I didn't want to be in the same room with God. I walked on eggshells, never knowing if I was going to encounter the loving God or the angry God. At some point, I believed that God would give me a list of the ways I'd failed him and would cut off any further relationship with me.

Yet I still wanted to believe in God, wanted to follow Jesus, wanted to be a "good" Christian, and a good son. I knew I was supposed to pray, but I was afraid to come close to God because I was afraid of what he might say to me. I was sure that God was just as disappointed in me as I was in myself, and so my prayer became a list of requests. Like a fast-food drive-thru, I'd put in my order and quickly move on, because I didn't want to hear God say something about my many failures.

But it's impossible to hear the true heartbeat of God if we are convinced that God's only messages are condemning and negative, making us so afraid that we keep our distance. In order to draw near to the heart of God, we first need to see the unhealthy ways that we think about and relate to God and where they come from. Simone Pacot guides us, saying that "Healing calls us to return to the parental . . . relationships, becoming aware of the way any wounds may have been infected. Then only is it possible to recognize that God is different from our father or mother, to renounce false ideas and then allow space to receive what God is saying."[47]

But before we can embark on this path of healing our heart theology, we have to face several other obstacles, for sometimes the theology that is connected with our experience of salvation reinforces the negative heart theology we received from our parents, which creates a toxic soup.

TOXIC THEOLOGY

As I shared in the previous chapter, I became a Christian as a teenager, after several years of listening to my Christian classmates tell me about Jesus and teaching me about the "end times." My foundational theology as an early Christian was that God was going to pour out his anger on the earth, but if I put my faith in Jesus, I would be forgiven and saved from God's wrath.

Though I was told that Jesus loved me and had "saved" me, I became afraid to come close to such an angry God. I knew that the moment before I had said "yes" to Jesus, God would have been ready to throw me—along with all the other sinners—into the torments of hell. So, Jesus wasn't only saving me from sin and death and the devil, but he was also saving me from God!

I certainly didn't want to be punished for my sin in the fires of hell, so I took Jesus up on his offer to save me, but I ended up with a theology that said, *Jesus is the good, loving Son,* and *God is a wrathful, punishing Father.*

This confusing combination of love and punishment combined with my heart theology made me reluctant to draw near to the heart of God, because the last thing I wanted to hear was what was on God's heart for me!

Eventually, I learned and received truly good news, which is that this is *not* the story that Jesus reveals about the Father. We'll return to this in the next chapter, but here I want to look at what Jesus reveals in his parable of the prodigal son.

> Jesus continued: "There was a man who had two sons. The younger one said to his father, 'Father, give me my share of the estate.' So, he divided his property between them. Not long after that, the younger son got together all he had, set off for a distant country and there squandered his wealth in wild living. After he had spent everything, there was a severe famine in that whole country, and he began to be in need. So, he went and hired himself out to a citizen of that country, who sent him to his fields to feed pigs. He longed to fill his stomach with the pods that the pigs were eating, but no one gave him anything. When he came to his senses, he said, 'How many of my father's hired servants have food to spare, and here I am starving to death! I will set out and go back to my father and say to him: Father, I have sinned against heaven and against you. I am no longer worthy to be called your son; make me like one of your hired servants.'
>
> "So, he got up and went to his father. But while he was still a long way off, his father saw him and was filled with compassion for him; he ran to his son, threw his arms around him and kissed him. The son said to him, 'Father, I have sinned against heaven and against you. I am no longer worthy to be called your son.'

"But the father said to his servants, 'Quick! Bring the best robe and put it on him. Put a ring on his finger and sandals on his feet. Bring the fattened calf and kill it. Let's have a feast and celebrate. For this son of mine was dead and is alive again; he was lost and is found.' So, they began to celebrate." (Luke 15:11–24)

In this parable, Jesus tells us that his Father is full of *grace* and *embrace*. When the rebellious son wishes that his father were dead and asks for his inheritance (somebody's got to die to get an inheritance), the father consents without question or condition. Next the son rebels, wasting the entire inheritance on the worst things. When he finally hits the bottom, he has a moment of clarity as he realizes that it would be better for him if he were a lowly servant in his father's house. So, he prepares his apology speech about not being worthy and heads for home.

But while he was still a long way off, his father saw him. . .

As I imagine it, *every* day since the son left, the father goes to the highest point in the village to see if his son is coming home. *Every* single day. When the son finally returns, the father is looking for him, as always, and he is so excited to see him that he *runs* to him! Jesus tells this parable to his followers so that we will know that *this* is what his father is like—persistent, even embarrassing, in his longing and his love for us.

In Romans 1, Paul describes the wrath of God as God *giving us over* to, consenting to, or *allowing* us to experience the consequences of our choices.[48] In Luke's parable of the prodigal son, the father *allows* the son to have the inheritance, and he *allows* the son to go and squander all that the father has given him. But after the father *allows* his son to bottom out and as he returns home, the father does not respond with anger or punishment, distance, or judgment, but he is "filled with compassion," and he runs to his son, embraces him, and kisses him.

As the son starts to deliver the speech he has prepared, the father interrupts him and immediately restores his sonship by giving him the ring and the robe. No questions, no conditions, no punishment, no lectures. He just wants "to celebrate" his son's return.

Melissa Helser invites us to experience this encounter with the Father's love in the spontaneous song, "Running Home":

You're the One Who's always running down my road.

You're the One Who's always running down my road.

Covering me with affection and clothing me in mercy. . .

It's not one time, not two times, not a hundred times.

It's thousands and thousands and thousands and thousands and thousands of times.[49]

Do we believe Jesus when he tells us that *this* is what his father is like?

For all the times that I heard and read about Jesus' love in my first twenty-one years of being a Christian, it didn't penetrate my heart and transform my beliefs about God's heart toward me. In my heart theology, the Father God would never run down the road to welcome me home. Instead, he was standing back at the house with his arms folded across his chest, watching me. As I crept cautiously up the driveway, he said, "Well, I'm glad you're home, but things are going to change before I let you back in the house. You are going to have to follow some rules."

I spent so many years being afraid of this Father God, but Jesus tells us that his father is full of compassion, delight (he ran!), and welcome (he embraced and kissed his son!).

For those who have had no father (or mother) or a bad father (or mother), or an average father (or mother), we have to overcome the obstacles and fortresses that the falsehoods have built around our hearts us so that we can trust the loving heart of God for our lives. As we journey into the goodness of God's heart for us, God is longing to heal us so that we can enter fully into the promise of life he has for us.

Our first step on this journey is to become *self-aware*. We need to return to those early years and remember the messages we received, how we interpreted them, and how we were impacted and shaped by our experiences.

In our work at Tierra Nueva with people in recovery we have used material known as *The Genesis Process*.[50] In *Genesis* becoming self-aware concerning the messages we received is essential as we work to uncover and bring healing to the unhealthy root systems that are producing the bad fruit of addiction in our lives. One tool *Genesis* uses has to do with the falsehoods we have built around our hearts by uncovering belief systems based on *projected lies* and *survival lies*.

Projected lies are those messages that were spoken to us and over us by people in authority in our lives. These could be statements like, "You're stupid," "You'll never amount to anything," "You're a victim." Our young selves hear these often enough and come to believe they must be true, and we live out of these beliefs.

Survival lies are those messages we have told ourselves to try to make sense of our negative experiences. They can be things like, "I will always be rejected," "Nothing ever works out for me," "I'm a failure," "I can't trust God." If we have experienced rejection, failure, and betrayal enough times, our minds develop these beliefs to help us make sense of those experiences.

All these *lies* contribute to our heart theology.

My heart theology, which was shaped by some of the negative messages that I received from my dad, included that God was an angry, disappointed judge, and I didn't feel safe drawing close to God's heart because I was afraid he would tell me how disappointed he was in me. I never questioned or examined this fear, but when the Holy Spirit began to show me these hidden places in my heart, I began to break through walls and long patterns of how I related to others and to God.

Our second step on this journey is to receive fresh revelation from Jesus about how the Father feels about us. We will explore this step in chapter 5, "Jesus Reveals the Heart of the Father."

Eventually, our healing and freedom will open space within us so that we can express the pain and anger we have stored within our hearts and then choose to forgive our parents. We will enter this work in chapter 6, "Heart Healing and Forgiveness." When we do not forgive others, we listen to the messages that our pain is telling, which warps what we are hearing from the heartbeat of God.

Simone Picot rightly points out that "this journey of truth can only be walked in the company of mercy; it's goal is an awakening to the areas of our lives that need conversion."[51]

Let us begin by taking the first step in our journey toward self-awareness.

ACTIVATION

Set aside some space and time to reflect on the relational dynamics you had with your father and/or mother (or other caregiver).

Find a place that is quiet and feels safe. Begin in silence, focusing on your breath. Acknowledge the presence of Jesus, who is with you always and will never leave you or forsake you. Continue to focus on your breath prayer.

When you are ready, think about your father, mother, or another significant caregiver. Take a moment to picture this person. Notice the feelings that come up in you. As you continue to take long, deep breaths, invite the Holy Spirit to reveal some of the relational dynamics from this caregiver that you might have transferred to God.

Take a moment to write these things in your journal. As you reflect, consider each of the following positive and negative attributes and think about where your caregiver lands. Move slowly and reflectively through the list.

Present	Absent
Affectionate	Distant
Involved	Uninterested
Attentive	Indifferent
Safe	Abusive
Promise keeper	Promise breaker
Generous	Stingy
Affirming and approving	Critical and dissatisfied
Strong and assertive	Passive and weak
Consistent	Unpredictable
Gracious	Unforgiving
Merciful	Condemning
Nurtured freedom, growth, and learning	Controlling
Genuine and sincere	Manipulative[52]

Now shift your thoughts toward your experience of God. As you return to the above list, consider how you relate to God and how you believe God relates to you. Try not to rush. When you are ready, invite God to reveal some of the "toxic" things you have taken from your earthly caregiver and projected onto him. Take a moment to record these things in your journal.

PRAYER

Heavenly Father, I confess that I have projected many unhealthy things on you. I trust that you know me and that you created me in love. I want to believe that you are different from my earthly father (mother). Holy Spirit, please plant the truth of God's love deep within my heart so that I can grow in God's love for me. Please deliver me from the false messages I have received and help me enter the fullness of the life you are imagining for me.

Chapter 5

JESUS REVEALS THE HEART OF THE FATHER

No one has ever seen God. It is God the only Son, who is close to the Father's heart, who has made Him known.

—John 1:18 (NRSV)

In a recent conversation with my spiritual director, he asked, "Do you think that God is as hard on you as you are on yourself?"

Sometimes I still think so—even after all the healing and freedom I have experienced. But most of the time, I believe that God is kinder, more gracious, loving, and merciful. While I've come to know that God is much better than I'd been told, I'm still on a journey of receiving the fullness of God's compassionate lovingkindness.

That journey has included my becoming aware of my heart theology and how my view of God has been shaped by my primary caregivers. The journey has also included a reformation of the theologies that lay the foundation to my faith, as some of these theologies were toxic.

With all this contributing to our view of God, it raises questions about how we can really know if we are hearing from the heart of God, for how can we say with confidence what God is *like*?

You may be thinking, "I know what God is like from the Bible, because it reveals the truth. 'God said it. I believe it. That settles it.'"

Yet throughout history, the Christian church has justified horrendous things by using the Bible—including slavery, racism, genocide, wars, violence, and the oppression of women. Moreover, the Bible is full of many conflicting images of God—some are violent, angry, and full of judgment, while others are gracious, merciful, compassionate, and full of welcome, embrace, and healing.

Because our hearts and minds have been shaped by so many early voices and experiences in our lives, those things will inevitably influence how we *hear* and interpret the Bible, and the heart of God revealed there. As we read Scripture, we may find ourselves feeling confused about what God is like or what we think God might want to say to us. As we seek to listen to God's heart for our lives, we may wonder how we can we know which images to accept as truthful and which to set aside because they don't reflect the true heart of God. Though we may accept the Bible as our primary source of revelation about God, we may still find ourselves wondering, "But what is God really like and how does God feel about *me*?"

In this chapter, we will explore how we can come to know and trust that the heart of the Father *looks, sounds,* and *feels* like *Jesus*.[53]

For Jesus not only came to inaugurate the kingdom of God, deliver us from darkness, rescue us from the path of sin and death, heal our "bad hearts and broken ways,"[54] and show us the path of forgiveness and new life—but Jesus also came to *reveal* the heart of his Father to the world. As the Gospel of John puts it, "No one has ever seen God. It is God the only Son, who is close to the Father's heart, who has made Him known" (1:18).

One pastor, author, and theologian who has profoundly shaped my thinking about how we can know what God is like is Brian Zahnd. As he puts it:

> God is like Jesus.
>
> God has always been like Jesus.
>
> There has never been a time when God was not like Jesus.
>
> We have not always known what God is like—
>
> But now we do.[55]

JESUS REVEALS WHAT GOD IS LIKE

When my wife and I first came to Tierra Nueva in the spring of 2008, I was in a place of significant transition. For the previous few years, it had felt as though God had ushered me into a room of expectant faith that felt larger than anything I'd ever been in or believed possible. Now as God awakened within me a deeper desire to know his heart and a longing to experience more of the Holy Spirit, it seemed I was being drawn into a room so large that it didn't seem to have any walls or a ceiling. In this massive space, my understanding of God felt untethered.

When Bob Ekblad interviewed me about coming to Tierra Nueva, I said, "I'm not sure I know what the gospel is right now. It's in pieces on the ground around me, and I can pick up a piece and say, 'I think this is part of it,' but I don't know how it all fits together." Though I don't recommend such a response for an interview for a pastoral position, Bob responded, "I feel so safe with you."

In those early years at Tierra Nueva, I felt as if I was in a theological crisis every other month. My nice, neat boxes of what God was like and how God worked in the world were being challenged and overturned. Prior to that, if you had asked me what I thought about Christianity, I would have replied with a line you might have heard: *Christianity is not a religion, it's a relationship.* By this I meant that Christianity wasn't about keeping a list of rules, but about knowing Jesus. The Gospel of John makes this point when he says, "the Law came through Moses, but grace and truth came through Jesus Christ" (1:17).

But when I peeled back the layers of what I really believed, I discovered that beneath my relationship with Jesus, there were a lot of rules about right beliefs and right behaviors that governed that relationship. This realization revealed that I had more of the Law-keeping heart of Moses than the grace and truth heart of Jesus. My understanding about God was still rooted in my heart theology, which had been shaped by the theologies of my formative years.

I experienced these theological crises whenever I encountered other staff or people in our community with whom I disagreed theologically or morally. Even though their *beliefs* didn't line up with what I thought about

Jesus or other aspects of theology, I could see the Holy Spirit working through them in beautiful and powerful ways, setting people free and bringing healing. And I was working with incarcerated and addicted people who loved Jesus, and yet their *behaviors* had landed them in jail and patterns of addiction. Yet when I prayed for them, I felt a firehose of God's love for them that was not offended by their behaviors.

These experiences made me wonder if God wasn't as concerned about people's beliefs and behaviors as I was. I started to think, *Maybe God isn't as hard on me as I think he is.* To my surprise, I was discovering (as my co-worker, Chris, often said) that "Jesus is better than we've been told."

Still, it was hard for me to shake the conflicting images of God I found in the Bible, where it seemed as if the God of the Old Testament and Jesus in the New Testament were two different Gods—an angry Old Testament Father and a loving New Testament Jesus.

During our Bible studies at the jail, Bob Ekblad regularly asked us to think about how the God portrayed to us by Jesus is different than the God portrayed by the Pharisees (or another religious representative in the Old or New Testament). As I reflected on this question, I noticed that my thinking was more like the Pharisees than Jesus, and this helped me begin to realize that *Jesus* reveals what God is really like.

The Gospel of John tells us this very thing, saying that "no one has seen God at any time," but "God the only Son, who is in the arms of the Father, He has *explained* Him" (1:18 (NAS), emphasis added). So if we want to know what God is like, and we want God's heart *explained* to us, we just need to look at Jesus, who is fully God and is the full expression of God's unchanging heart.

This astounding proclamation is not limited to the Gospels. The Apostle Paul, who initially persecuted Christians for saying that Jesus was God, began proclaiming the divinity of Christ after his mysterious encounter with Jesus on the road to Damascus (Acts 9:3–6). In Paul's letter to the Philippians, he writes:

> Christ Jesus, who, though he was in the form of God, did not count equality with God a thing to be grasped, but emptied himself, by taking the form of a servant, being born in the likeness of men. And being found in human form, he humbled

himself by becoming obedient to the point of death, even death on a cross. (Phil 2:6–8)

This passage, which is referred to as the *kenosis* (self-emptying) of God, is not simply an explanation of what God *did* in Jesus by giving up all the advantages of being God (such as being all-powerful, all-knowing, and all-present everywhere at the same time). Rather, Jesus reveals the very nature of God in his humble, self-giving love and his willingness to lay his life down for others. For God's self-giving love was not only expressed once on the cross or only in the incarnation of Jesus; rather, self-giving love is fundamental to *who* God is, always has been, and will be for all eternity.

In Paul's letter to the Colossians, he describes Jesus as the very "image of the invisible God" (1:15), emphasizing that "in him the whole fullness of the deity dwells bodily" (2:9). Before Paul's conversion, he would have considered such statements to be blasphemous and would have executed those who uttered them. Yet after Paul's Damascus-road conversion, he not only believed that Jesus was the singular, spectacular revelation of God, but he was also willing to be imprisoned and even be put to death for this stunning truth.

We must absorb these vital truths so that our theologies, ideologies, experiences, and mindsets can be transformed by the deepening knowledge that the fullest expression of God is revealed in the self-giving love of Christ.

JESUS IS THE FULL REVELATION OF GOD

We often operate as if we believe that the heart of the Father is really about the Law, about performing and obeying rules— withholding and punishing us when we don't. From this perspective, we imagine the Father as a judge, keeping law and order in the universe.

In contrast, as the Gospel of John tells us, Jesus reveals the heart of the Father *with grace and truth* as opposed to the Law that came through Moses (1:17), which suggests that ultimately, Moses (and the Law he brought) does not reveal the heart of God.

One of our regular Bible studies at Tierra Nueva from Mark 9 highlights this difference between the Law of Moses and the grace and truth of Jesus:

> And after six days Jesus took with him Peter and James and John and led them up a high mountain by themselves. And he was transfigured before them, and his clothes became radiant, intensely white, as no one on earth could bleach them. And there appeared to them Elijah with Moses, and they were talking with Jesus. And Peter said to Jesus, "Rabbi, it is good that we are here. Let us make three tents, one for you and one for Moses and one for Elijah." For he did not know what to say, for they were terrified. And a cloud overshadowed them, and a voice came out of the cloud, "This is my beloved Son; listen to him." And suddenly, looking around, they no longer saw anyone with them but Jesus only." (9:2–8)

This passage identifies Moses as the representative of the Old Testament Law and Elijah as the representative of the Old Testament prophetic tradition. Peter must have been blown away that his Rabbi was transfigured alongside these twin peaks of Jewish belief: the Law and the Prophets! Convinced that Jesus really was the Messiah, Peter started making plans to build three tents to honor these three great leaders.

But the Father interrupts Peter's grandiose ambitions, for suddenly a cloud covers them, and then a voice from heaven says, "This is My beloved Son. Listen *to him!*"[56] (emphasis added) Rather than placing Jesus on the same level as Moses and Elijah, the Father instructs Peter to listen to Jesus *over and above* the Law and the Prophets. While the Law and the prophets point toward Jesus, they are not the revelation of the Father, but Jesus is.

The author of Hebrews makes a similar point, writing that "in the past God spoke to our fathers by the prophets . . . but in these last days he has spoken to us by his Son," who "is the radiance of the glory of God and the exact imprint of his nature" (1:1–3). Moreover, the revelation of God in the Son is far greater than any former revelation, for Jesus is superior to the angels (1:4–14; 2:5), and superior to Moses (3:3–6), and he is the high priest of a better covenant (8:6–7).

Before I went through this Bible study on Mark 9 with my friends Tierra Nueva, I had read the Bible as a flat theological document, where all truth was equal and all Scripture had equal weight. Similar to the claims of holy books such as the Qu'ran or the Book of Mormon (where one author was said to receive the entire text as a revelation from God), I'd read the Bible as if it had dropped out of heaven in one piece, every word infallible and without error, each word carrying the same weight of truth.

But if we read the Bible as a flat text, where all truth is equal, then we might see the conflicting images of God as equal revelations of the Father, and we hear all the conflicting voices as if each was pulsing with the heartbeat of God. But when we see Jesus as the fullest revelation of God, we must understand everything else in the light of him.

As Brian Zahnd reminds us:

> God is like Jesus.
>
> God has always been like Jesus.
>
> There has never been a time when God was not like Jesus.
>
> We have not always known what God is like—
>
> But now we do.[57]

There is a theological term that describes God as *immutable*, which means *unchanging*. That means that Jesus didn't reveal something new that wasn't already in God, as if the "angry God" in the Old Testament suddenly *changed* to a "loving Jesus" in the New Testament.

Though God doesn't change, our theologies may need to be overturned, and our unhealthy interpretations may need to be healed before we can receive the unchanging, self-giving love of God. This has been critical for me as I have tried to discern whether something I am hearing is from God or from some other source. I have begun to ask myself, *"Does it look, sound, and feel like Jesus?"*

I'd missed the texts that highlight the supremacy of Jesus as "the image of the invisible God," in whom "the fullness of deity dwells bodily" (Col 1:15; 2:9) over and above many Old Testament images. And I'd missed the ways that Jesus, himself, overturned, expanded, and corrected the Old Testament interpretations about the nature of God.

JESUS OVERTURNS UNHEALTHY INTERPRETATIONS ABOUT GOD

God continues to speak to us through the Old Testament, for these were the sacred Scriptures of the early church. When Paul tells Timothy that "all Scripture is breathed out by God and profitable for teaching, for reproof, for correction, and for training in righteousness" (2 Tim 3:16), he is talking about what we call the Old Testament. These were the authoritative Scriptures for Jesus, yet he gives us a new lens for interpreting those Scriptures, just as he did for the disciples on the road to Emmaus on Easter morning: "And beginning with Moses and all the Prophets, he *interpreted* to them in all the Scriptures the things *concerning himself*" (Luke 24:13–35, emphasis added). That new lens is Jesus, himself.

Jesus radically reinterpreted the Scriptures for his disciples, saying, "You have heard that it was said, 'You shall love your neighbor and hate your enemy.' *But I say to you,* 'Love your enemies and pray for those who persecute you.'" (Matt 5:43-44, emphasis added). When Jesus was teaching, he redirected his followers from rigid obedience to Jewish Law to God's foundational heart, saying, "Moses gave you that... because of the hardness of your hearts, but it was not so in the beginning" (Matt 19:8).

A common theology in Israel during Jesus' day was that God blessed the righteous and cursed the sinners. We see this in the disciples' understanding of God in John 9: "As [Jesus] passed by, he saw a man blind from birth. And his disciples asked him, "Rabbi, who sinned, this man or his parents, that he was born blind?"" (vv. 1–2). The disciples interpret the man's blindness as a curse, which must be the result of God punishing sin (whether his or his parents).

For the Israelites, this theology was rooted in Deuteronomy 28, which says that if you do right, you will be blessed, but if you do wrong, you will be cursed. Anything that looks like a curse must mean you've done something wrong and God is punishing. We see other biblical writers wrestling with this theology in the book of Job and Psalm 73. We still wrestle with this line of thinking whenever we ask, "Why do bad things happen to good people?"

The Pharisees (the religious sect that tried to follow all the rules in the Mosaic Law) set much of the religious tone in Israel during Jesus' lifetime, and their theology was rooted in Deuteronomy 28. They believed that Israel couldn't receive God's blessing unless they did what was right, followed the rules and offered all the proper sacrifices when they didn't. They also believed that the long-awaited Messiah wouldn't come until everyone followed the rules and stopped sinning. In the light of this, every sickness, affliction, and demonic infestation was interpreted as God's punishment for sin, glaring evidence that Israel was still being cursed by God for its disobedience. And so the Pharisees sought to follow the 613 commandments of the Torah (Mitzvot) and developed an additional 39 categories of activity (Melakhot) prohibited on the Sabbath, in order to remain in the blessing of God.

But wherever Jesus went, he challenged, undermined, and overturned this theology. Every time Jesus broke the Sabbath, healed someone, cast out an evil spirit, or had a meal with "sinners" and outcasts, he revealed the true heart of his Father. If sickness, demonization, and being unclean and outcast were the will of God as a punishment for sin, then Jesus' actions would have been opposed to the will of the Father. But Jesus and the Father are *one* (John 10:30). Jesus overturned the theology that says, "sin separates us from God, because he is too holy to look upon sin or come close to it." Instead of saying that sin must be punished, Jesus revealed that God comes *near* to sin and to sinners because "it is the sick who need a physician" (Mark 2:17). Jesus' entire ministry was a correction to the theology of his day!

I was reoriented to this truth in jail, where I was part of a chaplaincy team for thirteen years, where I often heard a version of Deuteronomy 28 saying that *everything happens for a reason.* They usually meant that because God was in control and made everything happen, whatever we were experiencing must be from God and happening to teach us a lesson or punish us for our sins. Beneath this, I sensed a desire for the universe to make some sort of sense and to answer the "why" question, but there was also an underlying fatalism and Santa Claus theology.

Then Bob would interrupt this line of thinking and ask, "If the Pharisees represent what God is like, how would you describe God?" They'd say, "judge," "prosecuting attorney," "police officer," "parole officer." Then we'd look at Jesus spending time with "sinners" and coming close to outcasts, so freely forgiving and extending grace that he was mockingly called a "Friend of sinners."[58] And Bob would ask, "If Jesus shows us what God is like, how would you describe God?"

In the jail and on the streets, my theologies started to be upended.

In Bob's book, *Reading the Bible with the Damned*, I encountered the idea that it is critical for us to read the Bible with people from the margins for our *mutual liberation*. In other words, as we get out of our bubbles and see Scripture through the eyes of people who are different than us, especially people whose lives are more like the people who Jesus spent most of his time with, we will see the Bible and Jesus with new eyes.

In the process of facilitating this change in thinking with inmates, gang members, and addicts, who were often convinced that they were being punished by God, my own beliefs (such as, "God is as hard on me as I am on myself") began to be overturned by the goodness and mercy of Jesus.

When we see Jesus in the Gospels, we see the Father. And when we seek to hear the heartbeat of God in Jesus, "who is close to the Father's heart," in our lives and stories, he will upend false images and overturn theologies so that he can make "the Father known" to us (John 1:18). Jesus *is* better than we've been told.

REPENT AND BELIEVE THE GOOD NEWS

I have often wondered about Jesus' inaugural statement, "The Kingdom of God is at hand; repent and believe the good news" (Matt 4:17). Most teaching I've heard about repenting focuses on the need to stop sinning and live differently. "Repent" is often described as a command to turn away *from* something and turn *toward* something else—a 180-degree turn. While I have certainly done this regarding issues of sin in my life, I wonder if Jesus is inviting people to have a *new mind* about his Father and a *new imagination* for his kingdom. The Greek word for "repent" is *metanoia*, which is often understood to mean, "to have a new mind or think differently" about something. Perhaps Jesus' command to repent is an invitation toward a new understanding of God and new insights about what he wants to reveal in Jesus.

We will only live differently once we begin to think or believe differently. I believe that God wants us to repent of believing in a "loving Jesus, angry Father," so that we can receive the good news that God is one—Father, Son, and Holy Spirit—and come to know the love of the Father, which is fully expressed in Jesus and poured into our hearts by the Holy Spirit.

> God is like Jesus.
>
> God has always been like Jesus.
>
> There has never been a time when God was not like Jesus.
>
> We have not always known what God is like—
>
> But now we do.[59]

MY JOURNEY TO THE FATHER

I've already shared how my relationship with my dad impacted my relationship with God. As my theology began to be reformed by studying the Bible with jail inmates, my relationship with my heavenly Father also began to change. During this time, I heard a teaching on John 14, where Jesus says that "no one comes to the Father except through Me" (vv. 6–7). At the end of the service, the speaker invited us to pray and to ask Jesus to bring us to the Father.

As I began to ask Jesus to bring me to his Father during my prayer time each day, I found myself drawn to trust the heart of the Father more.

Several months later, as my wife, Susan, and I were praying for a young woman with deep childhood wounds in her family, I found myself praying for the first time to God the Father rather than Jesus. After we finished praying, I realized that something had shifted in me, for when I thought of the things I loved about Jesus, I now experienced love for the Father for those things as well.

As I began to feel stirred to direct my prayers to the Father, I asked Jesus if he minded. I had a sense of him laughing, and I thought, "Of course, there is no jealousy in the Trinity!" Then I thought, "whatever I say to the Father, I am saying to Jesus."

Jesus and the Father are One.

ACTIVATION

I am still walking this journey, as there are still *orphaned* places within me that need the healing love of the Father. Because of your own upbringing and wounding, and also because of your theology, you may feel that you don't know how to access a place of intimacy with the Father's heart. In the following activation, invite Jesus to take you by the hand and lead you to his Father. This path has already been walked by Jesus, and so it is covered with his footsteps of grace.

Find a quiet place where you feel safe and comfortable. As you quiet yourself, take a slow, deep breath and then exhale. Inhale again and thank Jesus that he is with you. Exhale and thank Jesus that he will never leave you or cast you out.

When you are ready, breathe in, *Jesus.*

Breathe out, *bring me to the Father.*

Breathe in, *Jesus.*

Breathe out, *bring me to the Father.*

Over the next several weeks, find ways to weave this breath prayer into your regular routine. Also, pay attention to people Jesus brings into your life to help guide you in this area.

Chapter 6

HEART HEALING AND FORGIVENESS

"To forgive is to set a prisoner free and to discover that the prisoner was you."

Lewis B. Smedes, *Forgive & Forget*

Even though I have experienced much healing and freedom in my interior life, I can still feel disconnected from God at times and can interpret God's silence as distance, telling myself that God is silent because I've done something wrong, or haven't done what he wants, or am not fully surrendered. I assume that God is giving me the silent treatment until I fall in line.

Though I know in my head that these messages come from *me*, not God, my heart doesn't always make that connection.

When I feel this disconnect, I often turn to the psalms. Reading Psalm 42 awakens my own longing, "My soul thirsts for God, for the living God. When shall I come and appear before God?" Or as I pray through Psalm 27, I feel an ache of pain rise in me as I read, "You have said, 'Seek My Face.' My heart says to You, 'Your face Lord, do I seek.' Hide not Your face from me. Turn not Your servant away in anger . . . Cast me not off; forsake me not" (vv. 8–9). This prayer often mirrors my feelings and has become the cry of my heart.

During one of those periods of silent disconnect, as I was reading verse 10, "For my father and my mother have forsaken me, but the Lord will take me in," my heart grieved for the ways my dad had forsaken me.

Even though I believed that the Lord had taken me in, some place deep within me still feared that God that would eventually forsake me and turn his back on me.

Whenever I realize how my relationship with my dad is still impacting my relationship with God, I know that I have more forgiveness work to do, another layer to uncover, orphaned places deep within me that continue to need the healing love of our Father.

Selah

As we seek to hear the heartbeat of God, we will encounter this stubborn obstacle again and again. As Simone Pacot puts it, "Healing calls us to return to the parental . . . relationships, becoming aware of the way any wounds may have been infected. Then only is it possible to recognize that *God is different from our father or mother,* to renounce false ideas and then allow space to receive what God is saying."[60] (emphasis mine)

As I've already noted, my ways of viewing God were shaped by my relationship with my earthly father as well as foundational theologies in my spiritual formation. Growing up, I imagined God as a judge who measured me by my performance and was regularly disappointed in me. I didn't feel safe coming close to God, because I was pretty sure he was going to say everything negative that I already believed about myself. I was so sure that he would punish me that I didn't question or examine this belief. It functioned as my operating system.

If we have been wounded by bent systems of belief because of our imperfect parents and early childhood experiences, how can we catch a glimpse of our true Father, who looks, acts, and feels like Jesus?

In chapter 4, "Heart Theology," I suggested we start by being honest about the dynamics we grew up with and mentioned pastor Rich Villodas, who describes these early dynamics as scripts. As he writes in *The Deeply Formed Life*:

> Scripts are the messages we receive, the roles we are given, and the ways we believe we must live that have been consciously handed to us or subconsciously interpreted by us. . . . When examining our family of origin formations, the naming of scripts provides interior revelation and positions us for the new scripts of the gospel.[61]

Not only do we have interior work to do, but we also need to get in touch with "the new scripts of the gospel," so that what Jesus reveals about his Father can transform our understanding of God and how he feels about us (as discussed in the previous chapter).

But there comes a point when moving forward means we need to forgive our fathers and mothers.

My heart theology operating system included a deep sense of failure and shame, which led at times to depression and despair, as I believed that God was as disappointed in me as I was in myself. I didn't want to stay in such a system, and yet I still had some faith deep within me that said, "Where else would I go? You have the words of eternal life."[62] But at the same time, that "eternal" life did not seem to be like good news.

As with my other friends in recovery, my movement toward truth, health, and freedom didn't come until I'd bottomed out, deeply stuck in the mire, and the pain of staying in my situation was worse than the pain of the work required for change.

As I mentioned in chapter 3, "A Journey into God's Heart," during the summer of 2000, a friend suggested that I read *The Bondage Breaker* by Neil Anderson. This book helped me begin to change my thinking and guided me onto the path of healing, deliverance, and freedom. As obstacles were removed in my relationship with God, I began to experience God's goodness and to sense that I had a tangible friendship with Jesus. The appendix of Anderson's book includes guided prayer work, which he calls, "Seven Steps to Freedom in Christ." That work includes praying through a variety of issues,[63] culminating in a section on forgiving those who have wronged us.

Jesus makes a specific point about forgiveness in the prayer he taught his disciples to pray: "Forgive us our sins, *as we forgive those who have sinned against us.*"[64] Yet as often as I'd prayed the "Lord's prayer," I had never really given much thought to forgiving those who had wronged me. I tended to think of sin in terms of my own wrongs—not those of others against me.

As I sought to connect with God and know his heart for me, I realized that forgiving my dad was a critical piece in healing and transforming my heart theology.

WHAT FORGIVENESS IS *NOT*

In spite of this realization, several things kept me from forgiving my father for some time.

First, I felt that if I forgave my dad (or anyone else), I was letting them off the hook, saying that what they had done was okay, or sweeping it under the rug. How often had someone apologized to me and I'd responded with, "Never mind, it's okay." Yet when I looked at Jesus, I saw that his forgiveness takes sin very seriously. He went to the cross because of his great love for us *while we were still sinners.*[65] Instead of sweeping sin under the rug, the work of forgiveness names the wrong and the hurt, but it removes us as the judge and hands the person who has wronged us over to God. Paul Young paints a vivid picture of this in his novel, *The Shack*, as his protagonist wrestles with forgiving an abuser. "Papa" God tells him, "It is about letting go of another person's throat."[66]

Second, I felt stuck because I thought that I had to convince my dad (or someone else) that he had wronged me before I could forgive him. I was waiting for him to apologize or confess the ways he had wronged me before forgiving him. But if we wait for this kind of acknowledgment, we may never be free. Those who have wronged us may never admit it—particularly if they have died, or we are estranged from them, or if we do not feel safe around them.

But as I found with my dad, the initial work of forgiveness involved me simply bringing him and my experience of pain to Jesus in my heart. Moving beyond forgiveness to the work of reconciliation would require both me and my dad to own our wrongs, to forgive one another, and to make amends. But I could forgive my dad, even if he never apologized or acknowledged the ways he had hurt me.

As I contemplated the work of forgiveness, I didn't *feel* like forgiving my dad, but I knew that I needed to *choose* to forgive him if I was going to experience healing and freedom. Forgiveness is not a feeling, but an act of my will to pray, "Jesus, I choose to forgive my dad for . . ."

For a long time, I tried to "forgive and forget." My dad would often tell me that time would heal all wounds, but time had never healed him or me. It just buried the pain until the next incident dug it up again. We don't forget. We repress.

After I did the initial work of forgiving my dad, I would continue to remember hurtful incidents, and then old feelings of hurt would rise up within me again. So I would go through the process of forgiving him again—and again. Each time, the process took a bit less time and involved less struggle.

Lin Button, teaching at a Healing Prayer School at Tierra Nueva, once said, "Forgiveness is the most powerful and, perhaps, least satisfying thing Jesus calls us to do. We may have to forgive the same person for one thing 490 times before it feels complete in us."[67] (The number 490 refers to Jesus telling Peter that he needed to forgive someone seven times seventy times.)

In *Experiencing Healing Prayer*, Rick Richardson speaks of this ongoing process of forgiveness, noting that "As we grow more mature and go deeper with God and others, we uncover new dimensions of our need to forgive and be forgiven. Forgiveness, then, is a process with crucial moments along the way."[68]

WHAT FORGIVENESS *Is*

Forgiveness work is a kind of spiritual surgery, and in order to remove the tumors of resentment and bitterness that keep us in bondage, it is important to be as specific as possible about the ways we have experienced wounding from others in terms of *actual sins, perceived sins,* and the *debts* we feel that someone owes us.

Actual sins are someone's words and actions that wound us in some way. These words and actions are obvious, and with parents and people close to us, they may include things that they *didn't do*, which we needed them to do. We may have experienced a lack of comfort or support or presence.

Perceived sins are when we believe that someone has said or done something that hurts us, and we later find out that we were mistaken. Until we discover the truth, we experience a wound that we need to address through forgiveness. Similarly, we may tell ourselves stories about our experiences with our parents that we do not remember accurately. We may have no idea what was going on for our parents at the time or what their true motives were. Even though our interpretations may be incorrect, our hearts still experience wounding, and this needs to be healed through forgiveness.

Forgiving *debts* can sometimes be more challenging than forgiving sin, because debts are connected to the idea of justice. A debt is what we believe the one who has wronged us owes us. While I grew up learning the Lord's Prayer as saying, "Forgive us our trespasses as we forgive those who trespass against us," the gospel of Matthew says, "Forgive us our debts, as we forgive our debtors." Some debts might include, "You owe me an apology," "You need to make this right," or "You need to change." Rick Richardson takes the list of debts even deeper, encouraging us "to let go of the debt we were owed, whether a debt of love, nurture, affirmation, or protection."[69]

When I have done forgiveness work in my heart towards others, I may still hold onto a sense that they need to change. While change may be required for the health of our relationship and for reconciliation, it is not required for forgiveness. When I realize that I am stuck, willing to forgive sin but not debt, I sense Jesus asking me, "How is that working out for you?" For when I choose to forgive both sin and debt, I feel a sense of release and new freedom. Perhaps when we release those who "owe" us something from debt, we free them to move toward the reconciliation we desire.

When I accompany people who are praying through forgiveness work, many are hesitant to name the wrongs done to them by their parents. For some, this may be connected to the fifth commandment, "honor your mother and your father,"[70] where naming sins feels like it would dishonor them. Others excuse their parents' actions, saying that their parents didn't mean to hurt them or that they were doing the best they could with what they had at the time. While these things may be true, if your parents sinned against you, you will need to forgive them.

As I have walked with people who have come from backgrounds of horrific abuse, there comes a point when their own healing and freedom will need to involve forgiving those who abused them. As Richardson describes this process, "When we forgive the sins against us, however terrible, we come out from being controlled by their effects. Jesus begins to deliver [us] from the destructive power of the person who has harmed [us]."[71]

WHAT DOES FORGIVENESS LOOK LIKE?

Several years ago, a young man asked me if I could pray with him about issues he was having regarding anger, which was having a disastrous impact on his marriage and his relationship with his children. We talked for a while and then prayed for the Holy Spirit to show us the root of his anger. He began to tell me about his relationship with his dad and shared that, growing up, he had been physically beaten by his dad almost every day.

After listening and asking some questions, I ventured, "I can only imagine what that was like for you, and you may not be ready for this, but I wonder if you have ever been able to forgive your dad for his abuse?" He told me matter-of-factly that he had.

I acknowledged the difficulty of that process and asked if he'd ever imagined forgiveness as taking his father to court and reading out the list of charges he had against his father and telling him how his actions made him feel.

He looked at me, eyes wide, and said, "No, I haven't done anything like that."

I invited him to imagine his father standing before him in a court room.

"That doesn't feel very safe," he shared.

Then I invited the young man to imagine Jesus as his advocate, standing between him and his father.

After a few moments, I invited him to speak out what his father had done (or not done) to hurt him and then to name how he *felt* in response to that wrong. The young man wept as he expressed his hurt and anger toward his father.

After he finished his list of charges, I invited him to *choose*, as an act of his will, to forgive his father and to hand him over to Jesus. After forgiving his father, the young man confessed his own anger and violence toward his wife and children.

Naming the wrongs *and the pain* brought healing for this man and his family and reminded me how important it has been for me to go beyond words of forgiveness toward my father and to express the emotional impact. While we may speak words of forgiveness, it won't make a difference in our inner landscape, because it doesn't touch our wounded hearts. But as Richardson describes the work of heart forgiveness, when we "see Jesus towering over [our] parents . . . greater than them, greater than any problem [we] face,"[72] we can freely express our pain and anger, and then we can "choose to forgive, to let go of the debt owed [us] . . . [and to] confess the sinful ways [we] responded."[73] This work continues to be part of my process.

Selah

When I first approached my own forgiveness work after working through the steps to freedom in the appendix of Anderson's *The Bondage Breaker,* I wasn't thinking of my dad, but I knew that I was stuck and needed to forgive people if I wanted to be free. I prepared my list of people to forgive as I sat in a coffee shop, and as I looked down at the long list in front of me, I saw the first name at the top— "Dad"—and burst into tears. I quickly left the coffee shop and walked to a nearby park, and over the next several hours, I prayed and cried through two pages of names as I forgave everyone I felt had wronged me throughout my life.

This heart work brought an immediate release in my relationship with Jesus and began to transform how I related to God and how I believed the Father related to me. I felt like a huge burden had been lifted off my chest, as if a stone had been rolled away from the prison of my heart. A prisoner had been set free, and that prisoner was me.

TO RUSSIA WITH LOVE

In 2015, I travelled with Bob and Gracie Ekblad to Krasnoyarsk, Russia, where we taught and ministered to a gathering of churches and recovery houses on inner healing, physical healing, and spiritual freedom. On our first night, Maxím, the bishop of these churches, described Russia as a country of orphans and reported that more than 20 million men had died in World War II, leaving behind generations of children without fathers, who had raised the next generation without having been fathered themselves.

The next day, as I was praying and reflecting on Russia as a country of orphans, I found myself thinking about how God had been meeting me in my own orphan experience. Later that morning, Bob asked me to teach on the Father's heart for Russia, and that night I shared what God had been shaping in me about the Father's heart for us. I shared that a primary obstacle is unforgiveness toward our earthly fathers, and I invited everyone to begin the process of forgiveness.

The following day, Maxím asked me to speak and minister at a prayer gathering in one of the recovery houses. After that meeting, I was approached by a woman in her thirties. Through a translator, she explained that her dad had never wanted her and that he had tried to kill her while her mother was pregnant, because he didn't want a baby to ruin his life. When that attempt was unsuccessful, he abandoned her and her mother. Years later, when she was thirty, she tracked him down. He rejected her and wanted nothing to do with her because he didn't want her to ruin his life. She had no idea how to forgive him and spoke about him matter-of-factly, as if she had walled off the pain within her.

Stirred by the Holy Spirit, I offered to stand in the place of her father, so she could see and speak to a person. Then I prayed that the Father would let me represent her father and invited her to speak out her list of charges—her anger, pain, feelings of rejection, and how it all made her feel. She poured everything out at me, and as the representative of her father, I admitted the wrongs and asked her forgiveness. Then I invited her to choose to forgive me and to release me to Jesus. After she forgave me, as I was still standing in the place of her father, I sensed the Spirit prompting me to speak a blessing over her. I blessed her as a wanted pregnancy and a desired daughter. I blessed her as a young woman coming into adulthood as a person of beauty and value and worth. I blessed her as a gifted and capable adult who was making me proud. I blessed her to flourish and thrive as the daughter of a father who wants her, loves her, and delights in her.

We were all in tears as the evening ended, and though I didn't see her after that night, I continue to pray for God to bring healing to the wounded places of her heart and to restore her full identity as a beloved daughter.

ACTIVATION

This activation is a more involved prayer exercise that will lead us through the work of forgiveness. I encourage you to set aside a safe, quiet space and devote plenty of time to this exercise. If you feel you are not ready to do this work at this time, feel free to come back later.

If you feel stuck in the ways you imagine and relate to God and want to experience freedom and receive the abundance that God has for you, you will need to get rid of the obstacles of unforgiveness and the debts you feel your parents owe you.

When you are ready to hear more clearly what is on God's heart for you, take a moment to quiet yourself and acknowledge God's presence in you and with you as you pray the breath prayer: *Father, take us deeper in your love.* Pray this several times until you feel settled.

When you are ready, invite God to lead you into a conversation about forgiveness. You might pray the following prayer, adapting it as needed:

> *Holy Spirit, you know the ways that I have been sinned against by my parents. You are not defending them in asking me to forgive. You are taking what has happened very seriously so that I can be healed. I invite you to reveal the things that I need to forgive my parents for and ask you for your grace, as I can't do this work myself.*

Write down everything that comes to mind, without excusing your parents. You were wronged by the things that they did or didn't do, and so it is important to name these things clearly and to address the effects of those sins on your life.

When you have finished making your list, enter your prayerful imagination and bring your parents to Jesus. Picture Jesus towering over them and then speak out their names and read the list you have written. You might say, *Mom/Dad, you did_____.* After each wrong, express your hurt and anger. This painful work begins your heart healing.

When you have said saying everything you need to say, choose to forgive your parents, even though they do not deserve it. You might pray, *I forgive you for all these things. I forgive the debt I have felt you owe me. I release you to Jesus.*

Now invite the Holy Spirit to show you your sinful, broken responses to the sins of your parents. Acknowledge these sins as true and ask Jesus to forgive you and to come into your wounded places and bring healing and restoration. Close your eyes and give yourself space to picture him cleansing you and bringing you wholeness.

In closing, renounce[74] the lie that your heavenly Father acts in the harmful ways that you have named and renounce any toxic beliefs about the Father that are rooted in these places of wounding, which are hindering your relationship with God. You might pray the following:

> *Father God, I confess that I have believed lies about you. I renounce the belief that you are _____ because of the ways my parents treated me. I declare the truth that you are not like my parents.*
>
> *Jesus, bring me to the Father. Holy Spirit, give me an open heart to see God as the gracious and compassionate Father revealed in Jesus. Thank you for helping me to know you, trust you, and love you.*

Rest in this quiet, prayerful space and receive what the Holy Spirit wants to bring to you through this time.

PART II:

UPWARD

Chapter 7

YOUR HEART
ALREADY HEARS

"You are already hearing God in many ways, and they all count."

—Bradley Jersak

In previous chapters, we've gone inward to become more aware of the clutter that can filter *what* we hear from God's heart. We may feel daunted as we try to clear all that clutter away, but God will help us.

In Hebrews we are told that "the word of God is living and active, sharper than any two-edged sword, piercing to the division of soul and of spirit, of joints and of marrow, and discerning the thoughts and intentions of the heart" (Heb 4:12). The "word of God" being described here isn't the Bible, but Jesus, the living Word. The living Jesus divides our soul (mind, will, emotions, and interpretations of our experiences) from our spirit (where we receive revelation from the Holy Spirit) to help us *discern* the thoughts and intentions of our hearts so that we can more clearly hear and understand God's heart. We will discuss the role of discernment in hearing God's heart later,[75] but in this chapter, we will explore *how* we can hear from God's heart.

Selah

Recently, a friend and I were taking a walk through his wooded neighborhood, and he stopped in front of a house and said he wanted to show me the pair of raccoons that frequented the area. He looked around but couldn't find them. "They must be gone," he surmised. Then I looked up and spotted them thirty feet above the house in a pine tree, hanging out on an exposed branch. "There they are!" I pointed. He looked up, but still couldn't see them. I directed his gaze with my finger, and then he finally saw them. "They're usually hanging out under the deck of the house," he explained. He'd had a hard time seeing them, because they weren't where he was *expecting* them to be.

In a similar way, as we seek to hear the heartbeat of God, we may *expect* to hear God speaking in a particular way or place. We may think that God will only talk to us in religious places, when we are doing religious things, and we may think that whatever God says will sound religious. Or we may expect God to speak to us only in obvious or familiar ways, a predictable repetition of what happens for other people. But if we limit ourselves to looking in one place for a particular word from God, we may miss all the other ways that Jesus, the living Word, is speaking to us.

We may also expect that when we "hear" God, we will hear a clear, distinct voice with our physical ears. God has spoken to me in many ways over the years, but I have only had a sense of him speaking strongly and clearly two times—and I'm still not sure how to describe what happened. Since hearing God audibly seems to be so rare, it might be more helpful to say that God *communicates* with our hearts in some manner, and we receive that communication.

As we consider some of the different ways that God communicates with us, we can be guided Scripture, which tells us that God speaks—and we can hear him. I want to begin by rooting our journey in a foundational promise from Jesus:

> But he who enters by the door is the shepherd of the sheep. To him the gatekeeper opens. The sheep hear his voice, and he calls his own sheep by name and leads them out. When he has brought out all his own, he goes before them, and the sheep follow him, for they know his voice. (John 10:2–4)

If Jesus is the Good Shepherd, and we are his sheep, and he calls each of us by name, then everyone can hear his voice. In *Can You Hear Me? Tuning in to the God Who Speaks*, Brad Jersak points out that Jesus does not say, "'My prophets hear My voice.'" Nor does he say, "'My pastors hear

My voice.'" And he also does not say, "'Only the spiritual people hear My voice.' But rather, 'My sheep hear My voice.'"[76] That means you, too!

Several years ago, I was hanging out with my friend Ryan, who was living in Tierra Nueva's ministry building at the time. Our friend, Marco[77], a former Latino gang member, joined us and then said, "I'm feeling closer to Jesus and I've been thinking I should get rid of my gun. Do you think I should toss it or sell it?"

Ryan smiled and responded with another question, "Why don't we ask Jesus what you should do?" So Ryan prayed, "Jesus, Marco has a gun. He wants to know whether he should toss it or sell it? What do you want to tell him?"

After a moment Marco exclaimed, "Oh mannnn!"

"What?" we asked.

"He said, 'Toss it.'"

As we talked about what it might look like to "toss it," I asked another question. "I wonder if Jesus wants to give you something in place of the gun?" So we prayed and asked Jesus.

"Oh mannnn!" Marco exclaimed again.

"What?" we asked.

"He said, 'It isn't weed.'"

After a pause, we dissolved into laughter. Marco had been thinking about selling his gun so he could buy marijuana, but Jesus spoke directly to him. Marco didn't use religious jargon but spoke honestly about what was going on in his heart, and Jesus met him there.

When we hear from God, our prayers become dynamic living encounters rather than static religious practices. While we won't always get immediate answers, our prayers become interactive. Rather than feeling like we're leaving messages on some voicemail in the sky or talking to the ceiling of an empty room, Jesus can become someone we are talking to right now, someone we can ask anything. Prayer becomes a real conversation we are having with a *living* and active friend, Jesus, the living Word.

GOD IS ALWAYS COMMUNICATING

The Bible tells us that God is always speaking and that we will hear him if we are listening. That promise isn't limited to what Jesus said in John 10, for God is communicating throughout the Scriptures, even though everyone may not be paying attention. As Elihu puts it in his rebuke of Job and Job's three counselors:

> Why do you complain that God answers none of man's words? God speaks, sometimes one way, sometimes another, even though you don't perceive it. In a dream, in a vision of the night. (Job 33:13–14)

When the word of the Lord comes to the prophet Jeremiah, God invites him to participate in the conversation, to ask and to listen: "Call to Me and I will answer you; and will tell you great and hidden things that you have not known" (Jer 33:3).

As Jesus promises his disciples, "The Helper, the Holy Spirit, whom the Father will send in my name, he will teach you all things and bring to your remembrance all that I have said to you" (John 14:26).

And later, Jesus continues: "I still have many things to say to you, but you cannot bear them now. When the Spirit of truth comes, he will guide you into all the truth, for he will not speak on his own authority, but whatever he hears he will speak, and he will declare to you the things that are to come" (John 16:12–13).

All these passages suggest that God has more to say to us than only the words written in the Bible, though any revelation will be consistent with the revelation of Jesus. As Brad Jersak explains, "Christ himself . . . the Revealer of the Father continues to reveal the Father in the power of the Spirit in existentially fresh ways for every generation of believers."[78]

If God has promised to speak to us, then we need to open our ears so that we can begin to recognize how we might have been hearing from God in ways that we have not yet perceived. As Brad Jersak puts it, "You are already hearing from God in many ways *and they all count!*"

REVELATION THROUGH INVITATION

The first way that many of us hear from God is through God's invitation to say "yes" to life with Jesus. For as Jesus teaches the Jews (who begin to grumble after he says that he "came down from heaven"): "No one can come to me unless the Father who sent me draws him (John 6:44). If you have come to a living faith through Christ, you are already hearing from God!

The invitation to enter life with Jesus may have come through a person, something we read, or some other experience, but God drew us, and we responded in our hearts.

When I was in high school, my friends invited me to various church events for over two years, encouraging me to have a relationship with Jesus. I went along with them, but I continued to resist. Eventually, I stood at the open door of that invitation to enter a life with Jesus, and I thought, "If God is real, he can handle my fears. If he is not real, then this prayer won't make any difference, so why not take the chance and pray?" That first conscious decision to step across the threshold into life with Jesus came after many invitations, which all originated in the heart of the Father.

Brad frames this initial invitation into life with Jesus as a pre-set channel on the radio of our heart, which picks up divine communication. Whenever we want, we can return to that channel and ask Jesus if he has an invitation for us today.

REVELATION THROUGH THE BIBLE

The church I was involved in during my twenties described the Holy Spirit as the silent partner in the Trinity, whose job was to point us to Jesus and help us understand the Bible—an understanding that seemed to suggest that the Holy Spirit was silent outside the Bible. Even though God can speak to us in many ways, which we will explore throughout this chapter, we need to ground everything that we hear in the biblical narrative and the revelation of Christ. God's written word isn't just a testimony about what God said and did thousands of years ago, for God continues to speak through the Bible to us today. Paul highlights this when he writes to Timothy: "All Scripture is God-breathed and is useful for teaching, rebuking, correcting, and training in righteousness. . ." (2 Tim 3:16).

The verse from Hebrews quoted earlier says that when the Word of God (Jesus) speaks to us through the word of God (the Bible), it is a *living* word from God's heart to us today. When we approach the Bible with expectancy, it can become a living, active word that can speak to us anew. Since God breathed upon it as it was first being written, we can ask God to breathe on it again as we read it today.

We experience this whenever we read a familiar Bible passage, and suddenly a word or phrase leaps off the page or speaks to a deep place in us. In these moments, God is communicating with us.

Or when we are thinking about someone or a situation, and we remember a particular Bible verse, or think of a Scripture without knowing what it says, God is speaking to us. I have a friend who hears from God in this way all the time. He will be driving to a meeting, and he will "hear" something like Joel 2:29, but he doesn't know what that verse says. When he gets to the meeting, he will look up the verse, and it always speaks to something he feels stirred to share in the meeting. In this way, God is communicating, and my friend is listening.

Sometimes the Bible can feel unwieldy and unapproachable, an ancient book that is difficult to understand, and so we avoid it, or we only read our favorite verses or whatever we come across on inspirational Instagram posts. Yet when we expect Jesus, the Living Word, to speak, we become attentive to how God can communicate to us right now.

In later chapters we will explore some ways that we can be more intentional about making space to hear God through Scripture.[79]

REVELATION THROUGH PEOPLE

When someone says something that speaks directly into a personal situation, as if the person has read our minds, God is speaking to us through that person. For example, whenever I prepare a sermon, I invite God to share his heart for the people who will be listening. Often, after preaching a sermon, someone will come up to me and ask if I'd been reading their journal, because I had spoken into a place of personal struggle or responded to questions they'd been asking. These encounters are mutually encouraging, for I have a sense that God is sharing his heart for others with me, and they are encouraged that God is listening to their prayers and responding to their questions.

We can also hear from God outside of religious gatherings or religious practices. In Numbers 22, God even speaks through a donkey! We can hear from God wherever we interact with people—coffee shop conversations, phone calls, emails, texts, and so on. James Martin, a Jesuit author, describes how he hears God in everyday conversations with friends. In *The Jesuit Guide to (Almost) Everything*, he says that "A friend may say something so insightful it is almost as if a window into your soul has just been opened: you may feel as if your friend's words are a way that God is communicating to you."[80]

Revelation through Books, Music, and Art

We could take the above quote from James Martin and replace the word "friend" with anything that opens "a window into [our] soul," such as music, books, and art.

When we read a book or hear music or see art that moves us deeply, touching our longing or flowing into a place of pain or joy, bringing tears to our eyes, the Spirit is opening our hearts to God's work in our lives. Rather than moving on from these moments, it is good to be still and soak in God's presence. God may be trying to speak to us, and as we make space to listen, we can invite him to reveal his heart to us.

For many years, as I struggled with fear in my life, God spoke to me through a character in Ursula Le Guin's science fiction novel, *The Left Hand of Darkness*. The two main characters in the book escape a Gulag-type imprisonment and travel across a vast arctic expanse of a frozen planet. They had planned their route carefully and knew that they had barely enough food to survive, but in the middle of their journey, they encounter an enormous cliff wall, thousands of feet tall, miles wide, blocking their way. Both are terrified of heights, but as they contemplate other routes that would bypass the cliff, they know that these would take them too far out of their path, and they would die of starvation and exposure. One morning, the narrator observes that his companion "favors the risk," "to stake life on the cruel quick test of the precipice," and he reflects:

> Fire and fear, good servants, bad lords. He makes fear serve him. I would have let fear lead me around by the long way. . . . What good seeking the safe course, on a journey such as this? There are senseless courses, which I shall not take; but there is no safe one.[81]

When I first read this novel, I didn't realize that God was speaking to me, but I wrote this passage in my journal almost daily for over a year: "I would have let fear lead me around by the long way." These words became a regular confession of sorts, reminding me that there is no "safe course" on the journey from fear and bondage into freedom and new life. Though the way might be perilous, I could make fear my *servant* rather than letting it lead me on "senseless courses."

REVELATION THROUGH A BURDEN TO PRAY OR ACT

When I invite God to reveal his heart to me, I try to pay attention to the thoughts that flit across the edge of my consciousness. Sometimes the thought seems so simple that I may dismiss it, but if I only look for something profound or miraculous, I may miss what God is saying.

Shortly after I first began to ask God what was on his heart for others, a couple came to mind each morning as I was making coffee. The husband was going through cancer treatments, and after I brought them to Jesus in my heart, I sent them an email to let them know.

They responded, "Oh Mike! This is so encouraging to both of us! [My husband] wants me to tell you how much we appreciate you telling us of the Holy Spirit prompting and of your prayers. Somehow it is now so much more personal and powerful." They went on to share what God was doing as they continued to pray for healing.

When we find ourselves thinking of someone, rather than letting that thought drift away, we can bring the person into our conversation with God.

Such momentary thoughts can carry a much greater impact than we might anticipate, going beyond encouragement to divine intervention.

In my work with Tierra Nueva, we accompany people affected by incarceration and addiction. I'd been walking with a man who was struggling with his new faith and his recovery, but he had withdrawn from our community, and I knew he was feeling isolated and depressed.

As I drove home from work one evening, I thought, "Call David."[82] I was tired and wanted to get some quiet time to myself, so I told myself I would call him later. But the thought came again, with more insistence, "CALL DAVID!"

So I punched his number, and when he answered, his voice sounded far off.

"David, what's up?" I asked. "Jesus told me to call you."

"Oh my God! I'm getting ready to kill myself!" he muttered, and then hung up.

I tried calling back many times, but he didn't answer. So I called 9-1-1 and then started calling people and asking them to pray. I called staff who knew David so they could reach out to him. Eventually, a police officer called and told me he had been able to contact David, but then David hung up and blocked his number. At least I knew he was still alive.

A few hours later, I was in an online prayer gathering, and as we were praying for David, he texted me: "When you called, I had worked up the courage to end it and had the machete at my throat. You and Jesus stopped me. I'm okay now." We ended up texting late into the night as God began to heal and restore him.

Later, David would remind me that prior to this encounter, I'd never called to say that *Jesus had told me* to call him. That piece of God's communication was foundational in re-establishing his relationship with the living Jesus, as he realized that Jesus was not merely a distant higher power but cared for him and wanted to be intimately involved in his life.

REVELATION THROUGH A CONVICTION OF SIN

Another time, as my friend Ramon and I were driving around our valley, running errands, he turned to me and said, "I've been thinking about how God convicts me." I invited him to share more. "I think when God convicts us, he's not pointing at us and saying, "You screwed* up!" (His language was more colorful than is appropriate here). "I think God is pointing to something in us and saying, 'I want to forgive that!'"

Ramon gave me a fresh way to understand how God is not looking for ways to condemn or shame us, but to forgive and restore us.

So often we confuse *conviction* with *condemnation*. God convicts us to point us toward reconciliation and restoration, healing and freedom, so that we can become who we are created to be in Jesus. But *condemnation* tears us down by shaming our identity. If we hear ourselves saying, "I'm a failure," that's condemnation. But *conviction* from the Spirit identifies something specific in our lives that needs healing and restoration. When we are convicted, we can say, "I failed in this way, and God is highlighting it so that I can own it and receive forgiveness."

God regularly convicts me as he firmly but tenderly brings to my mind areas where I need to repent—judgments in my heart, situations where resentment has settled in, or places of resistance in me. I know that God wants to set me free and lead me into greater joy and connection with him, and the Holy Spirit wants to remove any obstacles on that path, which might give the enemy a foothold in my life. As I confess these areas to God, the Spirit creates more room in me to experience God's love.

REVELATION THROUGH NATURE

Whenever we experience awe at the beauty and majesty of the earth, God is speaking to us. God often speaks to me about his nature through the ocean—its vastness and depth reminds me of the "height, depth, length and breadth"[83] of God's love. The Psalmist also hears God's voice in creation:

> The heavens declare the glory of God, and the sky above proclaims his handiwork. Day to day pours forth speech, and night to night

reveals knowledge. There is no speech, nor are there words, whose voice is not heard. Their voice goes out through all the earth, and their words to the end of the world. (Ps 19:1–4)

When we encounter places of great beauty—jagged mountains, storm-tossed oceans, rosy sunrises, ochre sunsets, bright autumn skies filled with light, stunning winter landscapes, vast rolling plains, golden mountain larch—and are stunned by the weight of the glory of the earth, God is communicating with us, giving us hearts to rejoice in all that we are receiving.

REVELATION THROUGH EMOTIONS AND FEELINGS

In *The Jesuit Guide to (Almost) Everything*, James Martin explores our "Friendship with God," highlighting how God can speak to us through our emotions, such as happiness, anger, "or sorrow over the plight of the poor."[84]

In worship gatherings, I sometimes find myself overcome with tears as I experience awe at the name of Jesus, or feel a tangible sense of God's deep love, or connect with God's heartbreak about a situation. Sometimes I don't know what my tears are connected to, but I don't cry often, and so when I do, I sense that God is communicating with me in some way. I have experienced a feeling of liquid joy being poured over my head, and I have been overcome by laughter from the Spirit. I have also felt unsettling things that seemed to be associated with a darker presence that God wanted me to be aware of in a space. And I have felt great grief over the many injustices and disasters happening in the world.

Through all these feelings, God is continually communicating with me.

Early in my faith journey, I was taught that we shouldn't trust our feelings, but should live by faith alone. Since then, I have come to understand that feelings are an important way God does communicate with us. I have also, at times, put too much emphasis on feeling the Holy Spirit, so I may think that the Holy Spirit isn't present, or active, or speaking to me whenever I am not "feeling" something. Pastor Rich Villodas offers a helpful corrective by clearly outlining the following three truths about the Holy Spirit and our feelings: "1) The Holy Spirit cannot be reduced to our feelings. 2) The Holy Spirit often speaks to us through our feelings. 3) The Holy Spirit is present even when we can't feel the Spirit's presence."[85]

REVELATION THROUGH INSIGHTS AND MEMORIES

Returning to *The Jesuit Guide to (Almost) Everything*, James Martin can help us pay attention to the variety of ways that God communicates with us: "Perhaps you're praying for clarity, and you receive an insight that allows you to see things in a new light . . . or you may, in a flash, perceive something surprising about God. . . . Memories also float to the surface in prayer." Then he asks, What is God saying to you through those consoling memories?"[86]

In 2005, the church where I was working in Seattle hosted a 24/7 prayer room.[87] For forty days, we had people praying every hour of every day in a designated prayer space in our building. During this creative, powerful time, we poured out our hearts to God as we prayed for our homes and city, seeking God's heart for us individually and as a community. At one point, we hosted a group from another church in our city, and two young men shared that God was telling them that I was going to be "a pastor to a church without walls."

I didn't know what this might mean in the context where I was involved, and when I asked Jesus about it, I didn't hear anything more. I wrote about this experience in my journal, and then I forgot about it.

Fifteen years later, on a Saturday morning in the Fall of 2020, this phrase, "you will be a pastor to a church without walls," rose up out of the recesses of my memory. I still wasn't sure what it meant, but as I prayed over the following weeks, pieces of clarity began to emerge.

The world was in the midst of the COVID pandemic that Fall, and most gathering places had been shut down. Online meeting places had exploded, and people were connecting outside the walls of the church. Since then, God has moved me into a new season of ministry with people all over the country and the world. I am now pastoring "a church without walls," and I can now see that in remembering this word, God was clarifying the shape of this time for me and the changes that were to come.

WE EACH HEAR DIFFERENTLY

As we consider the many ways that God is already communicating his heart with us, it is important to note that we don't all hear in the same ways. Rather than comparing ourselves with others, we can remember that we are each unique creations of God, and so God will speak to each of us uniquely.

I have a friend who "hears" God primarily through pictures, images, analogies, and metaphors. When she learned that her son was having a crisis of faith because he didn't "hear" God in the ways she described, she helped him see that her way of hearing didn't have to be his way of hearing. God speaks in many ways, and we can hear his voice in many ways!

Havilah Cunnington, the founder of Truth to Table, seeks to bring tools for discovering who God created us to be to our kitchen tables. One of those tools has to do with learning to hear God, and she describes four different ways that we might hear God's voice:

> *The Knower* is intuitive. You might just know you are supposed to go somewhere or do something but don't have a "word" or encounter to support the impression. *The Hearer* is likely to hear God saying specific things. Maybe it's a verse or word or phrase that comes to mind. *The Seer* is a visionary. God gives them pictures and images, some which may be so large as to cover a lifetime. *The Feeler* often senses God's communication through emotion.[88]

As you consider the ways that God is already speaking to you, it might be helpful to reflect on these categories to see if you hear in a primary way, but don't limit yourself to one. While I am primarily a *hearer*, I have also experienced God communicating through other avenues.

Sometimes we might have a profound encounter with God, but we often hear God's voice as a faint whisper. However God speaks to us, we are encountering the living Jesus!

ACTIVATION

In this exercise, we will reflect on the ways that we have already been hearing God. If you have some other people who are on this journey, I encourage you to do this in small group where the ways we are hearing can be affirmed and sharpened.

Take a moment to quiet yourself and welcome God's *always with you* presence.

Pay attention to the particular ways that you have heard from God in the past. Then invite the Holy Spirit to help you remember specific times when God spoke to you in that way. As you remember these moments of revelation, thank God for each one. When we give thanks, it waters the seeds of God's revelation that are already growing inside us.

In holding these seeds of revelation, ask the Holy Spirit if there is a primary way that God communicates with you, a pre-set channel of divine communication. Invite God to speak to you again in this way and to help you take time to listen and pay attention to his voice.

Chapter 8

A Heart We Can Only Imagine

"Supernatural ministry is weird by definition."

–Jordan Seng, *Miracle Work*

Now that we've taken time to notice the relatively "normal" ways that God communicates with us—thoughts, feelings, memories, music, nature, people, the Bible—I want to explore several of the supernatural ways that God speaks. Some of these may push the boundaries of our belief or challenge our sense of what we can expect of God.

Yet Jordan Seng's *Miracle Work: A Down-to-Earth Guide to Supernatural Ministries* gives an important corrective to the idea that the supernatural is beyond our belief, arguing that "the biggest problem among believers is not that we think supernatural ministries are too weird; it's that we try to make God seem normal."[89] Seng goes on to say:

> Think about it. We believe in an invisible being with no beginning who spoke the universe into existence; who lives outside space and time with fantastic angelic creatures; who is everywhere and knows everything and can do anything; who sent his God-man Son into our world, brought him back to life after he was thoroughly killed, and then returned him to heaven; and who resurrects us so we can live forever. Once you swallow all that overwhelmingly supernatural stuff, it's only the tiniest step

to accept supernatural healings and demonic deliverances—one drop in a whole bucket of weird.[90]

"JUST" YOUR IMAGINATION

To prepare ourselves to dive into that "bucket of weird," our first step off the "normal" path is to consider how God uses our imagination. The idea that we can use our imagination to interact with God might be an obstacle for some people, as we often grow up hearing that we need to draw a distinction between what is real or true and what is "just our imagination." Somewhere along the way, I picked up the idea that I shouldn't trust my imagination because it was not grounded in faith and the truth of Scripture.

A.W. Tozer, one of my favorite devotional authors, criticizes the use of the imagination, arguing: "Imagination is not faith. The two are not only different from, but stand in sharp opposition to, each other. Imagination projects unreal images and seeks to attach reality to them. Faith creates nothing; it simply reckons upon that which is already there."[91]

While I don't agree with Tozer, I understand his concern in trying to discern whether what we are hearing or experiencing is truly from God. If we use our imagination to make things up, how can it be a truthful platform where we interact with God?

In my journey toward embracing a *faith-filled imagination*, I had to come back to a foundational understanding in the biblical narrative, which is that we are created in the image of God (Gen 1:26-27). This means that Creator God created us with the capacity to *create*—not just to duplicate or mimic. Our imagination is the wellspring of the creativity of the Creator, in whose image we are created! Unlike God, the Creator, who created *ex nihilo* (out of nothing), we are co-creators with God, as we receive communication from the Holy Spirit. One of the avenues that the Spirit uses to communicate with us is our imagination, for it didn't come from some other source, but is part of what it means to be made in God's image.

Jesus intentionally engaged his listeners' imaginations through parables in order to reveal truths about the kingdom of God. He told us that we "must change (our) thinking and become like little children. If (we) don't do this, (we) will never enter God's kingdom" (Matt 18:3, ERV). Along with the easy trust of children, surely this includes an invitation to the childlike engagement of our imagination?

We know that our rational mind can't even encompass the fullness of the created and visible universe, let alone the invisible. Without our imagination, we could not, as Paul invites us, "look not to the things that are *seen*, but to the things that are *unseen*. For the things that are *seen* are transient, but the things that are *unseen* are eternal" (2 Cor 4:17–18, emphasis added). Brad Jersak suggests that the word *behold*, which appears well over a thousand times in the Bible, is an invitation to look with the spiritual eyes of our heart or imagination.

Morris Dirks, the founder of Soul Formation in Portland, Oregon, uses ancient Christian prayer practices as he works with leaders to help them connect more deeply with God's movements in their lives so they can operate from a place of knowing themselves fully loved instead of performing *for* love. In his exposition of the Ignatian Spiritual Exercises, Morris points out that "Ignatius believed that a primary pathway into the biblical texts and experiential encounter with Christ was through the use of imagination. . . . [The] active use of his imagination became fully developed as a tool to encounter Jesus."[92]

Though we sometimes use our imagination for questionable things, that is not the fault of our imagination—any more than it is the fault of our televisions for whatever we watch on them. God created us with a will, and with the ability to choose either good or ill, life or death.

We might think of our imagination as a screen that receives messages from the world (our familial, cultural, political, racial, and economic filters), from the flesh (our fears, fantasies, lies, self-defenses, and false beliefs about ourselves and God), from the devil, the "father of lies" (voices of accusation, despair, shame, condemnation), *and* from the Holy Spirit.

Our imagination was given to us by our Creator so that we can creatively interact with him. If God is up to things that are far beyond what we can think with the rational part of our brain, our imagination can be an avenue through which God will reveal his heart. In some of my deepest and richest encounters with God, I have prayerfully engaged my imagination to frame an intentional space to meet with Jesus.

In *Experiencing Healing Prayer*, Rick Richardson notes the importance of the imagination in his journey with God: "When I began to understand and embrace the crucial place of my imagination in worshiping and listening to God, my relationship with God underwent a quantum leap forward."[93]

In Ephesians 3:20–21, Paul proclaims, "Now to him who is able to do immeasurably more than all we ask or *imagine*, according to his power that is at work within us, to him be glory in the church and in Christ Jesus throughout all generations, for ever and ever! Amen" (NIV, emphasis added).

Because our thoughts cannot capture all that God wants to do in us and through us, we *need* our imagination! Earlier in this letter, Paul prays for the church in Ephesus to "have the *eyes* of [their] heart *enlightened*" (Ephesians 1:18, emphasis added). Paul is talking about *seeing* with our Spirit-filled eyes so that we can behold things that are beyond what we can ask or imagine. In this way of seeing, God's Spirit communicates with our spirit, and what we see by the Spirit is projected through our imagination, which is filled with God's light.

To give an example from our chaplaincy work in jails, we often talk with inmates about how God wants to heal them. We ask if anyone is experiencing pain, and as they indicate their various infirmities, we invite them to hold out their hands as instruments of the Holy Spirit for healing. We confess to God that our hands have been used for questionable things, and so we ask God to cleanse our hands and set them apart for his purposes. Then we ask for the presence of the Holy Spirit to be upon our hands, and we invite the inmates to put their hands on the places of pain in their bodies. God often brings healing in this way.

Similarly, we can pray and offer our imagination to the Holy Spirit. We can ask Jesus to cleanse our imagination of unclean things and then invite him to share his heart about the situation we are bringing to him.

Discerning what is truly from God and what is from other sources is critical work that we'll discuss further in chapter 11. For now, I will draw on an image from my friend Libby, who divides the work of hearing God into three buckets:

> If you hear, "I love you," "I want to be with you," or "You are so dear to me," you can just receive that. If you hear anything that sounds accusatory, anything that tears you down, anything shaming, that needs to be thrown out—or at least processed—because something is warping what you are hearing. And then there's everything in the middle. This is where we want to talk some more with Jesus and with others.[94]

An Open Door

When engaging in spiritual practices that activate our imagination, it can sometimes feel as if the interaction is self-generated or manufactured, because I am the initiator, the one setting the stage. My heart's desire is to have a real interaction with the living God, one that I can point to and say with confidence, "God said to me . . . God showed me . . . God revealed his heart to me . . ." But I often have to start by being intentional in my imagination in order to "prime the pump."

And sometimes, after engaging my imagination with my own thoughts and will, I come to a point when it becomes clear that I am no longer driving this bus. Something has shifted, and I am no longer imagining things on my own, but the Holy Spirit is communicating with my spirit.

To give one example, during a teaching at Tierra Nueva on listening prayer, Brad Jersak was leading us through an exercise he calls, "the Pearly Gates," which is based on the picture in Revelation 4:1: "Behold, there was a door standing open in heaven! And the first voice which I had heard speaking to me like a trumpet, said, 'Come up here . . .'"

He invited us to imagine prayerfully what that open door might look like. As I sought to quiet myself and open my imagination to God, I saw a large book lying open on the floor and thought, "This can't be right; it's not a door or gate." So I *tried* to imagine something else, but then Brad said, "It may not look like a gate or a door." So I returned to the image of the open book. Then Brad invited us to imagine Jesus meeting us there. *Where would he be? What is he doing? How does he greet you?*

I saw a man (who I assumed was Jesus) bent over this large book, which nearly reached his waist and was lying open on the ground. He turned as I approached, and a grin broke out on his face as he said, "I'm so glad you're here! I have so much to show you!" I had thought the book was the list of names in the book of life in heaven,[95] but I sensed I was seeing the Bible.

In my Spirit-guided imagination, Jesus took my hand, and we stepped up on the book. It was like we were standing on a clear surface, looking into a landscape of words and pictures. As we looked, we began to sink.

I watched this unfold in my imagination with childlike belief and curiosity. Then I heard Brad invite us to "picture Jesus' wounded hand and ask him to put it on a wounded place in you." Immediately, I saw a hand with a hole in front of me, and the hand clamped over my heart. I started crying, gasping for breath. For several minutes, I sensed Jesus doing deep healing in my heart. Though the exercise began in my imagination, God stepped in to lead me to a place of heart healing.

WHAT DO YOU SEE?

Throughout the Bible, God uses pictures, images, or scenes to communicate with his people. He asks the prophet Jeremiah, "What do you *see*?" (Jer 1:11–14, emphasis added). Jesus tells Nathaniel, "Before Philip called you, when you were under the fig tree, I *saw* you" (John 1:48, emphasis added). While exiled on the island of Patmos, John writes, "After this I *looked*, and *behold*, a door standing open in heaven!" (Rev 4:1, emphasis added)

In another exercise on hearing God's voice, we sat with a prayer partner. As we looked at our partner, we were invited to see the drawer in our kitchen that collects all the miscellaneous stuff—what we called "the junk drawer" in my family. Then we were invited to think about our partner and pay attention to anything that came to mind.

I pictured our junk drawer and noticed that it had a lot of refrigerator magnets in it. Our new fridge was made of some type of metal that magnets didn't stick to, and so the drawings, notes, and pictures that other families often put on a refrigerator were absent. I described this to my exercise partner, reflecting on how the magnets I saw in the drawer reminded me of the pictures of family or friends in ministry that I saw hanging on other people's refrigerators as reminders to pray for them. I wondered if the magnets in the drawer might be inviting my partner to enter into a season of prayer and intercession for people in ministry. My partner told me that this confirmed what he had been sensing God saying to him.

INTERPRETING DREAMS

Throughout the Bible, God communicates with people through dreams. In the book of Genesis, Joseph is known as a dreamer, who also interprets dreams. When two fellow prisoners ask Joseph to help interpret their dreams, he replies, "Do not interpretations belong to God? Please tell them to me" (Gen 40:8). Later, when he is brought before Pharaoh, he says,: "It has nothing to do with me; God will give Pharaoh an answer for his own good" (Gen 41:16). In Daniel, King Nebuchadnezzar has a dream, and Daniel prays and receives the interpretation for the king (Dan 2). In each case, God communicates through both the dream and the interpretation.

In the New Testament, an angel of the Lord appears to Joseph in a dream, instructing him, "Do not fear to take Mary as your wife, for what is conceived in her is from the Holy Spirit" (Matt 1:20). Later, Joseph is warned in a dream to go to Egypt (Matt 2:13–15). The Holy Spirit warns the Magi "not to return to Herod" in a dream (Matt 2:12). And when the Holy Spirit is poured out on all the people in Acts, Peter describes the interpretation of the event as a fulfillment of Joel (2:28–32), saying, "Your sons and daughters shall prophesy, and your young men shall see visions, and your old men *shall dream dreams*" (Acts 2:17, emphasis added).

Several friends have told me about how God regularly communicates with them through very vivid dreams. I typically don't remember my dreams, but I often remember details that seem to have a spiritual component and have come to believe that they are from God. Yet these details can be very strange and require discernment.

When I first came to work at Tierra Nueva, I dreamt that I was in a large, empty warehouse, and I saw two people coming toward me. I couldn't see their faces, but I heard a voice say, "These people are bringing Egyptian gods with them." Then the two people were standing right in front of me, and I started breakdancing. (That was an even stranger detail than the Egyptian gods!) Suddenly I was in a large, industrial kitchen, cleaning out large pots. A friend came in, and I described the first scene in my dream.

In other dreams, I have described the first part of a dream to someone later in the dream. In each case, I have dreamt about something that is happening or will happen. So I shared this dream with Bob Ekblad, and a week or so later, several of his friends from France came to Tierra Nueva to teach on liberation from evil spirits.[96] Bob asked me to tell them about my dream, and they shared that they had been involved in deliverance prayer in France with people from Egypt, who had brought demonic entities when they immigrated to France. Their deliverance had been very messy and still needed cleaning up (thus in my dream, I was cleaning pots in the kitchen). Just one more drop in a whole bucket of weird!

I still have no idea what some of my dreams mean. But whenever we have a vivid dream, whether recently or long ago, Brad Jersak suggests that we can "Step back into the dream and find Christ there. Ask him to tell you what each dream person and symbol represents. Ask him how he would like to resolve the dream and then watch what he does."[97]

VISIONS

God also communicates with us through visions, which involve the screen of our imagination, but bypass our creative agency. Visions are similar to dreams in that we do not consciously create them, but they occur when we are awake.

In Acts 10, Peter is on the roof of a house, praying and waiting for lunch to be prepared, when he falls into a trance and sees the heavens open and a great sheet, full of animals, being lowered. After the vision, "Peter was inwardly perplexed as to what the vision he had seen might mean" (Acts 10:17). As with dreams, visions are an initial communication from God, which require discernment for understanding.

My original Heart House encounter was a vision that came as I was praying. Visions have sometimes come to me in the space between waking and sleeping, where I have been semi-conscious, almost drifting off. In this liminal space, I seem to be more open to receiving what God may want to communicate with me.

In 2018 I was part of a team that was leading a *Dunamis*[98] conference on healing. One evening as the worship was winding down, I sat in the back of the room because I felt tired and disengaged. I started to doze off and, in the liminal space between sleeping and waking, I experienced a vision. Someone came to me and said that he had pain in his feet. Then he sat down on the ground, and others gathered around him to pray.

Suddenly I snapped awake, wondering what I was supposed to do with this vision.

At the front of the room, the pastor asked if anyone sensed God doing or saying anything for the group, and so I got up and went to the front and shared the vision. I wondered if God might want to heal anyone with feet issues, particularly *plantar fasciitis*, a term that came to me the moment I spoke it. Six people raised their hands, and so I invited others to gather around them to pray. As we agreed with God's healing in prayer, four people received immediate healing, including a woman who had previously suffered from a severed Achilles tendon, who started bouncing up and down on her toes—something she had not been able to do since the injury.

The content of such a vision is commonly called a *word of knowledge*, which comes from 1 Corinthians, where Paul lists the gifts of the Holy Spirit (12:8). A word of knowledge is a communication from God that contains specific information about a person or a situation, opening the door for that person to respond in faith. In this case, the word of knowledge was about pain in people's feet. The guidance in the vision to have people gathering around them to pray for healing might be considered a *word of wisdom*.

DIVINE MESSENGERS

The Bible is filled with stories about God communicating with people through angelic visitations. Angels appear throughout the Old Testament, and in the New Testament, angels communicate about Jesus' conception and birth (Luke 1:8–20; 1:26–38), and angels minister to Jesus after he is tempted in the wilderness (Matt 3:11). There are several angelic encounters in the book of Acts, as angels set the apostles free from prison (5:19–20), deliver a message to Cornelius (10:1–8), and set Peter free from prison (12:6–11). And angels are regular messengers in the book of Revelation. God continues to communicate with people through angels today.

Several years ago, the middle daughter of my friends was battling cancer, and their older daughter had a vision of an angel coming into the house, carrying a horn of plenty, and pouring something out on her younger sister. In the vision, she saw her sister's hair quickly grow back. Then the angel came to the older sister and poured out something that tasted, as she described it, "like peaches and hot sauce." Soon after this vision, her sister recovered, and she has been cancer-free for many years now. I shared this story with my small group and asked, "What kind of angel pours out peaches and hot sauce?!" My Hispanic friend laughed, "A Mexican angel!"

Another friend has told me about extraordinary encounters he has had with angelic messengers, who have given him explicit directions regarding prayer and spiritual warfare. Though this certainly stretches the boundaries of what we may think is "normal," it hasn't left the terrain we find in the Bible.

I have only had a few encounters with what I sensed to be divine messengers. But once, as I was experiencing a burnout point in my work with Tierra Nueva, I couldn't imagine continuing and wanted to quit. I had tried praying and taking time off, but nothing had changed. During this season, I started visiting a prayer room[99] near the airport in Bellingham, Washington to receive some focused prayer.

On one of these visits, as I made my way down the hallway to the waiting room for prayer appointments, I passed a new, seven-foot cross, which was mounted to the wall and backlit by a string of lights. As I stared at it, I reached out my hand to touch the wooden beam of the cross and felt peaceful and still. I stood there for a few minutes, not wanting to leave that place of rest.

Eventually, I felt stirred to kneel at the foot of the cross, and as I did, I had a vision of myself kneeling with my face pressed to the ground, and two angels came to me. One draped a blanket over me, and the other took something from a jar and wiped it on my mouth.

I was reminded of the story of the prophet Elijah, who runs for his life and comes under spiritual attack (1 Kgs 19:4–8). Burned out by his ministry, he asks God to take his life. After falling asleep in exhaustion under a juniper tree, he is awakened by an angel, who tells him to get up and eat. He eats the cake and drinks the water prepared for him by the angel, and then he goes back to sleep. The angel wakes him a second time and tells him to eat because the journey was too much for him. So he gets up and eats and drinks, and the strength of that meal carries him for forty days and forty nights until he reaches a cave on the top of a mountain, a safe place where he encounters God.

After recalling Elijah's story, I got up off the floor and was startled to see a woman standing in the hallway, watching me. "I don't know what you might think of this," she began, "but I just saw a large angel standing in the cross, and you were kneeling in the angel." I wasn't surprised, as her words confirmed what I had felt, and so I thanked her and made my way to the waiting room. After writing in my journal for a little while, I went back to sit under the cross and soaked in the supernatural peace.

When the prayer team finally brought me into a room to pray for me, I realized that my despair and exhaustion had disappeared. So I said, "Maybe you can just bless what God is already doing."

The author of the letter to the Hebrews describes angels as "ministering spirits sent out to serve for the sake of those who will inherit salvation?" (Heb 1:14).

From my own experience, I know this to be true.

AN AUDIBLE VOICE

God communicates with us in many ways, sometimes through a voice that we hear with our physical ears—just as if we are talking with a friend. God speaks in an audible voice throughout the Bible, as when God speaks to Moses through the burning bush (Exod 3:2–7), and God continues to speak to us today.

I've heard an audible voice speaking to me on two occasions. In the first, I was a freshman in college and was at the weekly college fellowship at my church, where a couple of cool looking guys talked to us about summer mission opportunities. My conception of missionaries was pretty narrow and stiff, and these guys challenged those ideas.

As I listened to them speak, I heard a voice ask, "Mike, would you do that for me?" I turned around, but there was no one was sitting behind me or near me. *Was God asking me to go on a mission trip?* I wondered. This encounter launched me on a journey of faith that took over a year and a half. Throughout that journey, I despaired at times, believing I had utterly failed God, but this audible question kept calling me back. God hadn't commanded me, but had asked me a question. I sensed that God was inviting me into a conversation. He did not simply want my obedience, but a friendship.

MEETING PLACES

Throughout the Bible, people encounter God in all sorts of meeting places.[100] The book of Exodus describes how "Moses used to take the tent and pitch it outside the camp, far off from the camp, and he called it the *tent of meeting*. And everyone who sought the Lord would go out to the tent of meeting which was outside the camp" (Exod 33:7, emphasis added). We can imagine ourselves stepping into a tent to meet with God, like Moses, or we can imagine another meeting place of our own.

My Heart House, which was given to me by the Holy Spirit, has become a primary *meeting place* for me with Jesus. One of my friends regularly imagines himself meeting with Jesus in a boat on a lake. Sometimes neither he nor Jesus say anything. They just enjoy being together.

The *meeting place* practice highlights how Jesus is the Good Shepherd, and each of his sheep can hear his voice, regardless of age, theological education, or experience in prayer.

When I first began meeting with Jesus regularly in this fashion, I had dinner with some friends, who shared that their thirteen-year-old daughter was preparing to make the move from homeschooling to public high school and was feeling anxious. I asked her if she'd like to hear what Jesus might have to say about the move, and she said yes. When I asked her to think of her favorite place where she could meet with Jesus, she imagined herself at her grandparents' island house, and Jesus was sitting with her on a log looking at the water. As she leaned against him, she felt very peaceful.

After she rested there, I invited her to ask Jesus if there was another place he wanted to meet her.

She told me that she was now flying with Jesus. As she adjusted to this new place, I invited her to ask Jesus why he was flying with her and what he wanted her to see or know through this experience. She admitted that she had a fear of heights and said that she sensed Jesus saying, "I want you to trust me." This interaction gave her a new confidence as she moved forward in her schooling.

As Brad encourages us, "If you have invited God into your life, there is a precious Person waiting there for you even now. Even if you have wandered from him, he has never left his home in your heart. . . . He calls all those with eyes to see and ears to hear to draw near—to behold and be held."[101]

In concluding this chapter, we will practice using the screen of our imaginations to create a *meeting place* where we can encounter Jesus.

ACTIVATION

These following questions are intended to guide you as you seek to imagine your own meeting place with Jesus. Take a few moments to quiet yourself, thanking God for his *always with you* presence. As with the activation from the previous chapter, this is a good exercise for a small group of people to experiment with God and discern together what God is saying.

> *Where do you feel drawn to meet with God? Take a few moments to imagine yourself in that place. How old are you? What are you doing?*
>
> *Now imagine God coming to meet you. How does he arrive? What does he look like? Is he coming to you as Jesus, a father, a friend? Where is he in your meeting place? What is he doing?*
>
> *What expression is on his face? What do you see in his eyes?*
>
> *What is the first thing he says to you? What do you say to him?*
>
> *When your conversation comes to an end, invite him to tell you how he feels about you.*
>
> *As you sense your time drawing to a close, ask Jesus if he has a promise or blessing for you.*[102]

Chapter 9

GIVING GOD
OUR ATTENTION

"God desires to communicate with you all the time, but when you intentionally open yourself up to God's voice, you can often hear it more clearly."

James Martin, SJ, *The Jesuit Guide to (Almost) Everything*[103]

Several years ago, my wife attended a conference in San Antonio, and I tagged along. I thought I could use the long weekend away to study and prepare for a class I was teaching on "treasure hunting," which is a practice of listening to and following the leading of the Holy Spirit. Kevin Dedman describes this practice in his book, *The Ultimate Treasure Hunt: A Guide to Supernatural Evangelism through Supernatural Encounters.*[104] Treasure hunting involves listening to who and what is on God's heart and then *going* to find that person to share it. The idea behind treasure hunting is that *everyone* is God's treasure, but many aren't yet aware of it. While we might agree that everyone is God's treasure, we can't interact with *all* people, and so we invite God to speak to us about specific people whom God wants us to find. Then we can go find them and bless them with whatever God is sharing—simple, but risky!

We start by asking the Holy Spirit for clues that will guide us to the specific person who God wants to reveal as his treasure. We might begin by asking, "Holy Spirit, will you give me clues that will lead me to the people you want to bless through me today?" After asking the Holy Spirit for clues, we write down some notes, which we might arrange into five categories: appearance, location, specific needs, names, and prophetic words.

Before stepping into this exercise, I suggest reading chapter 10, "Hearing God's Heart for Others: Partnership and Prophecy," as I highlight some important guidelines for how we can best share with others what God is sharing with us.

On my first morning in San Antonio, I spent some time in silence. As I prayed, I asked the Holy Spirit for clues, writing down the things that came to mind. Then I walked around the neighborhood on my way toward a coffee shop. I didn't see anyone who matched the clues I had written down, and I didn't push myself to go out of the way, so I spent the day reading and writing in the coffee shop.

The next morning, I tried again. As I prayed and listened, I pictured myself sitting in the coffee shop at the same table as the day before. In the picture I saw a brown-skinned man with black hair and a blue shirt sit down at the table next to me. I thought, "John," and then, "right arm." So I wrote down these clues, put the piece of paper in my pack and headed out.

As I sat in the coffee shop drinking my coffee and writing, people came and went from the table next to me. Then I looked up and saw a man with brown skin, dark hair, and a blue shirt come in and sit at that table. A few moments later, another man came in to meet him. The man stood and introduced himself as *John*. After a short meeting, the second man left, and John remained.

I took the risk. "Excuse me. Did I hear you say your name is John?"

"Yes."

"This is probably going to sound weird," I began (my standard intro), "but I was praying this morning, and I asked God for clues about the person he wanted to bless and, well, let me show you."

I reached into my pack, pulled out my piece of paper with the clues, and handed it to him. He scanned it and said, "This sounds like me." I asked him if he had any problem with his right arm. "No," he said. "It's my right foot. But it's a limb—does that count?"

We laughed, and I told him that the first thing God wanted him to know was that he was God's beloved son and God was delighted with him. His shoulders drooped as he sighed and said, "That's really hard to believe."

"I know!" I responded. "We are so wired for performance in every relationship. We get a job because of how we've performed in other places. We keep that job or get a promotion because of how we've performed in the job. Even our closest relationships have an element of performance. But our relationship with the Father is one of being loved by him before we've done anything—no performance!"

We spent the next hour and half talking about all the ways he was wrestling, including the struggles his wife was having. She had been mad at God ever since her miscarriage. The doctor had told her she wouldn't have any more children, and she'd had chronic headaches ever since. After listening, I shared that a name very close to hers had been on my list from the day before, along with *headaches*. I offered to pray for him and for healing in his wife's heart toward God and also in her body.

A few months later, he sent me an email and said that his wife was pregnant! We were both hugely encouraged!

BEING INTENTIONAL IN PRAYER

I have found it helpful to be intentional in giving God my attention by making space to listen to him through a variety of spiritual practices. The Jesuit author James Martin offers a helpful insight, reminding us that "God desires to communicate with [us] all the time, but when [we] intentionally open [ourself] up to God's voice, [we] can often hear it more clearly."[105]

While it is important to cultivate that space intentionally, we might be tempted to try to *make* something happen, as if God were at our beck and call. Being intentional is more about paying attention and opening our hearts to receive what God is already doing and imagining—not about trying to get God to do something.

Rich Villodas talks about this intentionality in terms of *contemplation*:

> To contemplate something is to fix your attention on it in a curious and deliberate manner. Contemplation is what happens when you fall in love. It's what happens when you catch a beautiful sunset. It's what overtakes us when beholding an exquisite piece of art. We were made to contemplate. But here's the thing: contemplation is not truly possible without a prolonged sense of attentiveness. Our pace must slow down. This is particularly difficult in a skimming and scrolling culture...

He elaborates, observing how, "Contemplative prayer is not just about our pace, but about space—in particular, our inner space. The person contemplating is not just a subject observing an object, but a subject being *encountered* by another Subject (God). In this act of mutual *beholding*, the defenses we have built up slowly come down as we open our 'inner space' to God's grace and love."[106] (emphasis added)

I love the images of being encountered by God and of mutual beholding. James Martin once pressed his mother about what happened when she prayed, and she said, "Well, I quiet myself down. And then I look at God, and God looks at me."[107]

In *Guerrilla Gospel: Reading the Bible for Liberation in the Power of the Spirit*, my friend and mentor Bob Ekblad talks about six practices he gleaned from the book of Habakkuk to help him intentionally seek to look at God and be encountered by him.[108] These six practices include: quiet yourself, focus on Jesus, ask questions (speaking complaints and requests), look for vision, tune into spontaneous thoughts and impressions, and finally, write it all down. I will briefly explore these six practices below.

Quiet Yourself

Because we are often distracted and our lives are filled with noise, we may not notice God speaking to us. This has been true for ages, as the psalmist hears God telling him to "be *still* and know that I AM God" and observes, "For God alone my soul waits *in silence*" (Ps 46:10, 62:1, emphasis added). Jesus directs us to go into our closet (a space set aside to be with God) and shut the door so that we can be in a secret place with God, our Father, who will reward us (Matt 6:6). One of those rewards is simply knowing that God is with us, whether we feel his presence or not. We open ourselves to hearing from God when we intentionally set aside space and time to be with him.

Cultivating stillness and silence are often the hardest spiritual disciplines, as they don't come naturally or easily to us. Rather, as *disciples*, we have to learn these *disciplines* through practice as we seek to develop muscle memory around regular sacred rhythms. Our purpose in cultivating these practices is not to convince God to do something through our efforts, but to create space within ourselves to receive what God is already doing so that we will be ready to notice it.

As I mentioned in chapter 1 in the introduction to breath prayer, when we first begin to practice being quiet, we will inevitably be distracted. But when we become aware that we are distracted, we can simply acknowledge it and then return to the center of our stillness. Though I sometimes feel as if I'm not making much progress, my wife reminds me that we are training ourselves to *return* (or repent) from our wanderings in the far country of our thoughts back to the embrace of the Father. This is the muscle memory we are building over the long haul.

Focus on Jesus

You may have a simple prayer that helps you connect with Jesus, such as, "Help me, Jesus," or, "Lord Jesus, have mercy on me." While my attempts to focus include these prayers, it has also helped me to spend time in musical worship, praise, and thanksgiving as a way of becoming more aware of his heart so that I can move my attention toward remembering all that Jesus has done in my life and give him thanks. Through this practice, my heart, mind, and spirit become more centered on Jesus. As the psalmist writes, "On the glorious splendor of Your majesty and on Your wondrous works, I will meditate" (Ps 145:5).

Sometimes we may pray or sing the words, "We magnify Your Name," as a way of intentionally expanding our vision, thoughts, hearts, and minds on Jesus. I notice that when there is something negative or stressful going on my life, if I focus on it, it seems to get even bigger. I *magnify* it! But instead of *magnifying* our stress, we can seek to *magnify* Jesus!

Ask Questions, Speaking Complaints and Requests

When we come to Jesus, we don't need to pretend that we're "all good" or that the world is "all good," for it is important for us to be completely honest with God about what is on our hearts, especially when we're burdened, struggling, or grieving. God already knows our hearts, so we should not pretend we're fine in the name of faith. As the prophet Habakkuk cries out, "How long, O Lord, will I call for help, and you will not hear?" (Hab 1:1).

However you come to Jesus, you can begin by sharing what is on your heart and then ask God to share his heart about the situation. You might pray, "Jesus, what is on your heart about this person or situation? What do you want me to know?" In speaking to the prophet Isaiah, the Lord describes a people who "draw near with their words, and honor Me with their lip service, but their heart is far away from Me, and their reverence consists of the commandment of men that is taught" (Isa 29:13, NASB). God does not want our praise to be words disconnected from our hearts.

Look for Vision

As we focus on Jesus and give voice to our complaints and questions, it is important to notice anything that catches our attention. What thoughts rise in us? What seems curious? As the prophet Habakkuk says, "I will *keep watch* to *see* what He will *say* to me . . . " (Hab 2:1–2). What do you *see* God *saying* to you?

During Moses' exile as a would-be liberator, he works as a field hand for his in-laws for forty years. While tending sheep, Moses *sees* a bush burning that isn't consumed (Exod 3). As he turns aside and looks *to see* what is happening, he has an encounter with God, who speaks to him and gives him a call that changes the course of history for Israel.

The prophet Jeremiah declares that the word of the Lord came to him and asked the same question twice: "'Jeremiah, what do you see?'" (Jer 1:11, 13). After the first question, Jeremiah sees an almond branch, possibly with his physical eyes. Then the Lord says, "You have seen well for I am *watching* over My word to perform it" (1:12). Note that in Hebrew, the word "almond" is very similar to the word "watching." After the second question, Jeremiah sees a boiling pot, tilting toward him from the north.

We don't know whether this is a natural or supernatural vision, but God declares that disaster will be coming from the north (1:14–16).

Our invitation is to continue to *look* to *see* what God will *say* to us in our time and our particular situations.

While writing this book, I sensed Jesus calling me into a new season.

While waiting in silence during this transitional season, God *showed* me the raised garden beds that I had planted in the alley behind our house filled with onions, kale, lettuce, arugula, sugar snap peas, tomatoes, potatoes, cucumbers, and zucchini. As I looked to *see* what he would *say* about this image, I found myself reflecting on how each year, I am overzealous in my planting. The seeds and starts are so small and seem to take up no room at all when I first plant them, and I plant too many so the beds will look full, but now the beds are overflowing, and plants are crowding each other out, and some are choked off and less fruitful.

As I continued to look to *see* what God would *say*, I sensed God inviting me not to be so overzealous in my planting in this new season. I recognized my temptation to say, "Yes," to too many things so that I would look and feel productive, and I sensed God inviting me to wait for his guidance about what and when to plant, paying careful attention to how each tiny plant is growing and what sort of space it requires before planting anything else.

Tune into Spontaneous Thoughts and Impressions

As we give our attention to God, it is important to notice any images, pictures, or words that come to mind. If we dismiss the first thing that comes to mind because it seems too simple—such as, *Jesus loves you*—we might not hear the particular word that God wants to reveal to our hearts.

To give another example, if you find yourself staring at someone's shoulder, God may be trying to get your attention because he wants you to pray for that person. Or if you feel uneasy about a decision you have made, God may be impressing you to reconsider. Wherever our thoughts lead us, it is important to ask God for more information about how he is leading us.

While walking through my neighborhood on a silent prayer walk one evening, a friend's name came to mind, and I felt a surge of anxiety that wasn't connected to anything going on in my life. I paid attention to this and began to pray that my friend would be "rooted and grounded in the Father's love," particularly around any anxiety. After my walk, I messaged my friend, who responded that she had been experiencing a sense of panic around a possible health scare and thanked me for sending the message, as it made her feel that she was on God's radar.

Write it Down

Journaling can help us grow in hearing and recognizing the voice of Jesus, the Good Shepherd. After we spend time looking and listening, we can take a moment to write down whatever we "see" or "hear." My journal is a place of wrestling, further conversation, and discernment. It is also a place of encouragement, for as I look over the record of my experiences of God speaking, I grow in my expectancy that God will continue to speak into my life. As the Lord tells the prophet Habakkuk, *"Record the vision and inscribe it on tablets, that the one who reads it may run. For the vision is yet for the appointed time; it will hasten toward the goal. If it seems to tarry, wait for it, it will surely come, it will not delay'* (Hab 2:2–3, emphasis added). I will talk more about journaling in the next section on listening to God in Scripture.

LISTENING TO GOD THROUGH SCRIPTURE

God promises us that he will communicate to us as we intentionally listen to what God is saying to us in the Bible. The following three practices have facilitated my ability to hear God in Scripture.

Journaling

First, we can listen to God through Scripture by journaling about whatever we are reading. As we read, we can invite the Holy Spirit to interact with us by praying, "Holy Spirit, make this word your living word! I need to hear from you today."

As we read, we can also ask God questions and give God thanks and praise. We might journal about what bothers us in the passages we are reading, what confuses us, or things we struggle with in the text. Pay attention to what rises in you as you express yourself. Imagine yourself having a conversation with Jesus and ask him what he wants you to *see* and *hear* as you read.

Once, when I was reading the story of the paralytic in Mark 2:1–12, I wrote to Jesus in my journal: "You know I love this passage. I've led Bible studies and preached on it. I already know what I think about it. What do you want me to know that I am missing?"

Immediately I had the thought, "They called me a blasphemer." This stopped me in my tracks. Jesus had done this amazing thing by healing the paralytic, but his teachings and actions were outside the accepted religious practices, and so the religious leaders *cancelled* him. As Jesus revealed this to me in my journaling, I became aware of my own religious boxes. As I thought about my own judgments regarding who was "in" or "out," I realized that I might have called Jesus a blasphemer, too.

Imaginative Contemplation

A second way to engage Scripture intentionally is by reading a text prayerfully and imaginatively. My spiritual direction supervisor is a former Jesuit, and I find his insight about the common Evangelical approach to Scripture helpful: "Evangelicals study the Word to learn *about* God. But Scripture is to be *experienced* so we can *encounter* God."

Ignatius Loyola, the founder of the Jesuit movement, described such experiential encounters as *imaginative contemplation*. He instructed his disciples to visualize Gospel texts in this way. In the United Kingdom, the Jesuit "Pray-As-You-Go" ministry offers recorded guided encounters into a handful of Gospel stories, explaining that "Imaginative contemplation is a way of getting to know and even meeting Christ in the Gospels. The ultimate goal is personal encounter with him. Take your time with this kind of prayer. God is in no rush."[109]

Lorie Martin describes a similar approach in her book *Invited: Simple Prayer Exercises for Solitude and Community*.[110] She invites us to read a text and make it a meeting place with Jesus. As we read, she encourages us to pay attention to the characters and ask ourselves whom we most identify with at this time and why we connect with this particular character.

Then she invites us to read the passage a second time and imagine it from this character's perspective, reflecting on what emerges in us as we identify with this character and how their experiences relate to our own life.

Finally, she invites us to read the passage a third time and reflect on where we sense God in this story. How does God feel toward us? How do we feel? What does God want to tell us or show us or make known to our heart? As we share our heart with God, how does God respond? She concludes by encouraging us to rest with God and receive whatever God has for us—and then give thanks.

Lectio Divina

A third way we can engage with Scripture is through the ancient practice of *Lectio Divina*, which is a way of slowly reading a short passage several times and listening to what the Spirit might be saying to us. Much has been written on this practice, but I have found Ruth Haley Barton's outline particularly helpful.[111]

> *Prepare*: Begin by taking a moment to still yourself and become fully present to God's presence with you. Express your willingness to hear from God. Affirm that he lives in you and is always with you. Spend time giving thanks as a way of tuning your heart to hear his voice.
>
> *Read and Listen*: As you read the chosen passage, read slowly, pausing between phrases and sentences, listening for a word or phrase that stands out and seems to be addressed to you. Allow a moment of silence, repeating the word or phrase. Don't judge or analyze it.
>
> *Reflect*: As you read the passage a second time, ask, "What in my life right now needs to hear this word?" Allow several moments of silence to reflect and explore thoughts, images, and sensory impressions.
>
> *Respond*: Read the passage a third time, feeling how you are responding to what you are hearing. Enter into conversation with God, talking about what is coming up in you. Pour out your heart in complete honesty.

Invite: As you read the passage a final time, invite God to respond to what you have shared. Ask the Holy Spirit, "What is your invitation to me from this word?" Continue to listen to this invitation throughout the day, inviting the Spirit to draw you deeper into it.

A few months ago, as I was preparing to enter this new season, I felt drawn towards Lectio Divina and asked Jesus to lead me to a passage. Immediately, I thought, John 3, but I resisted, because I was already familiar with that passage (as if I already knew everything there was to know!). I wanted to read something fresh, but I only heard silence, and so I trusted that Jesus had something to say to me from John 3.

I picked verses 5–9 and read them slowly. Then I read them again. The phrase that stood out was, "That which is born of flesh is flesh, and that which is born of the Spirit is spirit" (v. 6). I was at the beginning of a new season of work, starting from scratch, and I was feeling anxious to get busy and look productive. As I read this verse a third time, I talked with Jesus about my anxiety, and I sensed him telling me that my desire to be busy was born from my flesh and would not produce the fruit of the Spirit. As I sat with this passage, I confessed my temptation to look productive and thanked Jesus for his patience and his desire to see fruit born of the Spirit through my work. I asked him for grace to wait for his leading.

As we practice listening to God's heart through Scripture, we need to give ourselves permission to "get it wrong." For we are still *learners*, so we won't always hear "perfectly." As I noted in early chapters, our hearts can color what we think we are hearing—sometimes we might hear God's heart, sometimes we might hear reflections of our own brokenness, and sometimes we might hear voices from our culture and other sources. But when we *write down* whatever we hear, we can return to it later in order to discern what is from God and what is from our brokenness or culture.[112] Give yourself a lot of grace trust that God wants to share his heart with you!

ACTIVATION

This chapter is filled with several activations that can help you become more intentional about listening to God's heart. Before moving onto the next chapter, I invite you to work through at least one new practice from this chapter and see how God speaks to you. Remember to *write it down*! While Lectio and Imaginative Contemplation can be done on your own, they are also great practices to do in a group.

Chapter 10

GOD'S HEART FOR OTHERS: PARTNERSHIP AND PROPHECY

"Every believer is able to prophesy on an inspirational level, because we all have been filled with the Spirit of God."

—Graham Cooke, *Prophecy & Responsibility*

Several years ago, my wife and I were at the wedding of some friends who'd met later in life, and we ended up sitting next to a friend I'd known in college but hadn't seen for many years. I knew she'd been involved in Christian ministry but had since heard that she'd moved away from that as well as her relationship with God.

As we sat together, I invited Jesus to show me his heart for her, and I immediately had the thought, "Tell her that I love her just the way she is."

I resisted, because I worried that if she'd distanced herself from God, she would dismiss a simple statement like, "Jesus loves you." So I pressed Jesus for something more. "Give me something I couldn't know so that she will know it's from you!" I was hoping that "the secrets of [her] heart [would be] disclosed and so, falling on [her] face, [she would] worship God and declare that God is really among [us]" (1 Cor 14:25).

But I got radio silence from Jesus, and so I didn't say anything to my college friend.

Later at the reception, we were seated at the same table, and after everyone else got up to get food, I found us sitting alone together. I thought about Jesus' word for her, and so I looked over at her.

"What?!" she demanded.

I admitted to her that during the ceremony, I'd asked Jesus what was on his heart for her.

"Oh yeah?" she said sarcastically. "And what did he say?"

"He said, 'Tell her that I love her just the way she is.'"

Her eyes got very big, and then she rushed over and hugged me. In a desperate whisper, she said, "You have no idea how much I needed to hear that!"

She was right. I didn't have any idea. I had thought I needed to say something flashier and more specific that would pierce her heart, but Jesus had known exactly what she needed to hear.

From time to time, God continues to drop this friend's name on my heart out of nowhere, and I so I pray for her. If I get something particular to pray about, I'll drop her a message, and she'll respond that the timing and content of God's heart was very specific and important.

When we seek to hear God's heart *for others*, we are moving into what the Bible calls *prophecy*. In this chapter, I will focus on personal or inspirational prophecy, which is sharing God's heart for an individual person. Paul describes this as the *gift* of prophecy (1 Cor 12:8–11; 14:1–25), which is distinct from the *role* or *calling* of a prophet (1 Cor 12:29; Eph 4:11).

Whatever your experience with personal prophecy, which some people describe as a "word from the Lord," it is about *hearing God's heart for others*. We can hear from God for others in the same ways that we can hear from God for ourselves.

In exercising the gift of prophecy, God is inviting us to partner with him in seeking after his lost sheep, proclaiming his heart of love as he seeks to rescue people from the rule of darkness, proclaim good news to the poor, and deliver the captives. All around us, people are desperate to hear from the living Jesus, to know that they are seen, known, and loved.

The more I have sought to hear God's heart for me and to draw close to him, the more he has shared his heart for the hurting people around me.

The love and power that flows from God's heart isn't simply for our own delight and personal encouragement, for God wants to draw us outside of ourselves so that we love our neighbors just as we ourselves are loved. As Jesus puts it, "freely you have received, freely give" (Matt 10:8, NIV). God's intention has always been to fill us with his Spirit and to send us out to the ends of the earth *for others*. As I've heard Pastor Bill Johnson from Bethel Church in Redding, California put it, "The Holy Spirit is *in me* for my sake, but *on me* for yours."

In prophecy, we are talking about the Holy Spirit being poured out *on* us *for* the sake of others. As Jesus said, "'If anyone thirsts, let him come to me and drink. Whoever believes in me, as the Scripture has said, 'Out of his heart will flow streams of living water.' He said this about the Spirit, whom those who believed in him were to receive . . . .'" (John 7:37–39). The Holy Spirit is a stream of living water meant to be flowing *out of us* and *onto* others.

Let's consider Jesus' mission statement:

> "The Spirit of the Lord is upon me, because He has anointed me to proclaim good news to the poor. He has sent me to proclaim liberty to the captives and recovering of sight to the blind, to set at liberty those who are oppressed, to proclaim the year of the Lord's favor." (Luke 4:18–19)

Scripture says that the Spirit was *upon* Jesus and empowered him to speak words and do actions that brought about liberty for the captives, healing for the blind, and freedom for the oppressed. The Holy Spirit empowered Jesus throughout his earthly ministry, and then Jesus passes that onto all his followers, saying, "As the Father sent me, so I send you" (John 20:21).

We have the same mission as Jesus (apart from dying on the cross to overcome sin, death and the devil), and the same Spirit that was *upon* Jesus empowers us to do the same works that he did. For as Jesus proclaims:

Truly, truly, I say to you, whoever believes in me will also do the works that I do; and greater works than these will he do, because I am going to the Father. (John 14:12)

We are meant to operate from the same place as Jesus, fully surrendered to the Father, fully empowered by the Holy Spirit, fully engaged in bringing God's kingdom to earth as it is in heaven. When we co-labor with God, *good news* will be proclaimed to the broken, the hungry, the captive, the blind, and the oppressed. One of the ways we can proclaim this good news is to listen to God's heart for others—and then *share* it. This is prophecy!

ALL PLAY

I think we often disqualify ourselves from co-laboring with God because we think that *ministry* is something that "professional" Christians do up front during a church service on Sundays. This separation between "church ministry" and non-church callings in the workplace is not biblical, for God is constantly working in the world in many diverse ways—not only through church-sanctioned ministries and events held in church buildings.

Covid has revealed to all of us that the church is not about a building or what happens in that building. Rather, *we* are the church, and we are *all* invited to participate in God's ministry, wherever we are. We are temples of the Holy Spirit and the same Spirit that raised Jesus from the dead continues to live in us. That Spirit wants to flow like a river through us to the hungry and thirsty people we interact with all day long, wherever we are. The post-Covid church is a church without walls.

Throughout the Old Testament, God raised up leaders who performed various aspects of the "ministry" for the people—judges, prophets, priests, and kings. Those who were empowered (or anointed) by his Spirit were called to communicate God's heart to the people and to lead them according to God's ways. Yet if we limit ourselves to these Old Testament examples of the work of the Holy Spirit, we may quickly disqualify ourselves, assuming that we need to hold certain roles in the church, or live a good life, or attain a certain level of maturity in order to be empowered by the Spirit.

Yet to the prophet Joel, God promises, "I will pour out my Spirit *on all flesh.* Your sons and daughters shall prophesy, your old men shall dream dreams and your young men shall see visions. Even on the male and female servants in those days I will pour out my Spirit" (Joel 2:28–29, emphasis added).

This prophecy is fulfilled in Acts 2 when the Spirit is poured out on *all* who are gathered for the Pentecost feast (vv. 3–4). In the Old Testament, *particular* leaders were chosen by God to be empowered by the Spirit, but now we are invited to be part of an All Play.[113] *Everyone* is invited to listen to the Holy Spirit and to receive God's heart for others—not just leaders, or insiders, or mature believers, or those who have gotten their lives all cleaned up. In fact, God tells the prophet Joel that his Spirit will be poured out on *all* flesh, which includes servants, along with the voiceless and *all* who have been excluded and marginalized by political, cultural, and religious systems and structures.

During a fall retreat for Tierra Nueva's ministry staff, we engaged in a reflective reading of Scripture (Lectio Divina) and then sat together in silence. After several minutes, the director of our Migrant Chaplaincy shared that God had given him a Scripture reference that morning as he was driving to the retreat. He wasn't sure what the passage contained, but the verse he heard was Joel 2:29. We looked it up: "Even on my male and female servants in those days will I pour out my Spirit."

Through this verse, God highlighted his heart to pour out his Spirit *on female and male servants*—the marginalized, who have no rights, no voice, no place or value in society, who are often considered to be disposable. In our ministry context, we identified these people as inmates, addicts, gang members, homeless, prostitutes, migrant workers, First Nations, undocumented, and refugees. Upon these disinherited and marginalized people, God is pouring out his Spirit. *ALL PLAY!*

One Pentecost Sunday, I met with a woman named Lorinda in the garden space behind our ministry building. Lorinda had come to our church through New Earth Recovery, a local recovery house, after enduring a long journey with addiction and recovery, relapse, and re-recovery. She had spent three years living in a drug house, and while living in the recovery house, she had heard her daughter-in-law, Jessica, talking about Jesus and singing worship songs. She knew this was a radical change for Jessica, whose life had been dramatically transformed. Eventually, Lorinda came to church with Jessica and welcomed Jesus into her life and was baptized in the local river.

On that Sunday in May, as we talked about what it meant for the disciples in Acts to be filled with the Spirit and "speaking in tongues" (Acts 2:4), I shared some stories about how I'd see the Holy Spirit use this gift and asked her if she had any experience of it.

"No," she replied.

"Would you like to?" I asked.

"Yes!" she said with enthusiasm.

We prayed, and the river of the Holy Spirit began to flow out of her with this gift. She was so excited as she began to pray for people and situations out of this Spirit-inspired language, especially when her mind didn't know what to pray or ran out of words. As she has continued to exercise this gift, God has placed his heart for others on her heart, and in sharing these words with others, she has become a co-laborer with God!

FAITH INVOLVES R-I-S-K

The idea of partnering with the Holy Spirit in sharing God's heart for others may sound risky—and it is! Anytime we speak about what God might be saying, we are taking a risk, because we don't want to misrepresent God (a sign of humility), and we don't want to be wrong (a reflection of our pride).

Most of the time, when I invite God to share his heart with me, I receive a word or phrase for people with whom I have some level of relationship. Or sometimes someone I don't know approaches me during prayer and expresses a desire to hear from God. When someone approaches me to receive prayer, I feel more freedom to share, and yet I still want to be careful. So I usually begin by saying, "As I'm praying, this thought is coming to me . . . ." Then after sharing what I've heard, I ask, "Does that mean something to you?"

When I pay attention to a name that God drops on me, I often pray, "Father, take them deeper in your love." Sometimes, I sense that this prayer is enough. But other times, a subsequent thought will lead me to pray in a particular direction.

When I sense something particular, I often send a message, letting people know that the Holy Spirit "dropped" their name on me, and I share any specific prayer that came to mind. One friend responded by saying, "I truly do not know what to think about these promptings, but I just had the first genuine prayer I've had to start facing some really big fears—to move out of denial—in a good long while. Thank you for following these promptings, they are a lifeline to me in essential moments."

Though sending these messages always feels risky, it is both humbling and exciting to partner with God in encouraging someone and to experience the Holy Spirit as a stream of *living* water being poured out on someone who is thirsty.

Sharing with people we don't know is even more risky! Yet we are surrounded all day by people who may not have someone listening to God's heart on their behalf. How will they ever know what is on God's heart for them if we don't take the time to listen—and if we aren't willing to risk sharing what we hear from God's heart?

To give one example of sharing with a stranger, several years ago I was at the dentist to get my teethed cleaned. As I lay back in the chair, I asked God what was on his heart for the dental hygienist. The thought that came to me was, "She is not her mother."

I sat there, mulling it over, wondering what I was supposed to do with this word. I knew I couldn't dismiss it, because I never would have had that thought on my own, but I was afraid to risk saying anything.

When the hygienist finished my cleaning, we had to wait for the dentist to come in to check my teeth, and I began by saying, "This is probably going to sound really strange to you, but I'm a Christian, and as you were cleaning my teeth, I asked God what was on his heart for you, and the thought that came to me was, 'She is not her mother.' Does that mean anything to you?"

She paused thoughtfully and then said, "No, not really. People say I'm a lot like my mom and I think that is a good thing."

Swing and miss. The dentist came in, and the conversation ended.

. . . Six months later

I was back in the office for another cleaning. I was in a different room, but I had the same hygienist. As I lay back, I asked Jesus what was on his heart for her, and the thought that came to me was, "She is not her mother."

I tried to point out that the Spirit had been wrong six months before, but God didn't budge. "She is not her mother."

The hygienist finished the cleaning, and feeling foolish, I said, "I don't know if you remember me, but six months ago. . ."

"Oh, yes, I remember you," she responded.

"Does, 'She is not her mother,' mean anything now?"

"No. Not really."

"Come on Jesus!" I thought.

In the awkward silence, I looked around the room and noticed several pictures of a young boy hanging on the cabinets. "Those are great pictures," I said. "Is that your son?"

"Yes," she smiled. She paused and looked down.

"You know, my mom wasn't a very good mom. She wasn't around much and was gone a lot at work."

I ventured, "Are you worried that because you are a working mom and not around as much as you'd like, you aren't a good mom? I think Jesus wants you to know, 'You are not your mother.' You are a good mom."

She teared up, and several weeks later, I received the only thank you note I've ever had from a dental hygienist.

GUIDELINES FOR SHARING GOD'S HEART WITH OTHERS

Now that we've talked about the risk involved in sharing God's heart with people, it's important to talk about *how* we share what is on God's heart. God has given us some helpful guidance in Scripture.

God is Love

As I was learning more about the gifts of the Holy Spirit with a group of others, we read Paul's first letter to the Corinthian Christians. Chapter 12 discusses the supernatural ways that the Holy Spirit empowers the church, and it also addresses the problems that the community at Corinth encountered because of their sin and brokenness. Then chapter 14 talks about some more controversial gifts, such as prophecy and tongues, and how they are to operate in a healthy way in any gathering of God's people.

Chapter 13, which I had often thought of as the "wedding chapter" in the Bible, falls right between these chapters about the gifts of the Spirit in the church. But rather than being a detour from the supernatural stuff, 1 Corinthians 13 highlights *love* as the foundation of our partnership with the Holy Spirit:

> If I have prophetic powers, and understand all mysteries and all knowledge, and if I have all faith, so as to remove mountains, *but have not love*, I am nothing. (1 Cor 13:2, emphasis added)

Paul says that if the love of God for others is not the source of our prophecy or any other gift we are *nothing*—and would be better off *not saying anything*. In fact, he says that if God's love is not the source of our communication, we are just making a lot of noise: "If I speak in the tongues of men and of angels, but have not love, I am a noisy gong or a clanging cymbal" (1 Cor 13:1).

Moreover, he goes on to say that God's love keeps no record of wrongs (1 Cor 13:5). And God's love is neither prideful—as in, "look at what God is saying through me"—nor envious—as when we strain for a word from God so we can validate ourselves in comparison with others (v. 4). Moreover, God's love, as Jesus tells us, should even extend to our enemies (Matt 5:44).

Graham Cooke, a charismatic prophetic voice in the United States, highlights the necessity of love as our foundation: "To properly release the prophetic gift in our lives, we must remain in the love of God. We have to learn how to see people the way God sees them. Then we need to learn how to speak to people the way God would speak to them."[114]

Love is our primary guide. The heart of God is filled with irrepressible, unconditional love for the sinner, the weak, the enemy (Rom 5:6–10). The love of God runs down the road to gather us into his welcoming arms like the father of the prodigal son, over and over again. The love of God does not condemn and is never against us, but always *for* us. Is this love flowing through us as we listen? Are we tapping into this love before we speak? What is going on in our own hearts as we seek to share God's heart with others? Sometimes, we may need to remain silent, for without love, any words we share will just make a lot of clanging noise.

God Builds up, Encourages, and Comforts

As Paul writes in 1 Corinthians 14:3, "The one who prophesies speaks to people for their *upbuilding* and *encouragement* and *consolation*" (emphasis added). These three pillars should guide us as we seek to share God's heart with others. We might ask, *Will what I share build this person up (strengthen them)? Will it encourage them? Will it comfort them?* Sometimes we may only see a picture or have a sense about something rather than receiving specific words. Yet even if what we are hearing is not particularly clear, these questions can still guide us.

When we receive specific information about what is going on in a person's life, it is called a *word of knowledge*.[115] If we receive negative information, such as something the person is struggling with, Graham Cooke gives us important guidance: "Never give the first thing you receive; don't be in a hurry to prophesy . . . We can dialogue with God. 'Thank You Father. Now, in light of *that*, what is it You want to say to him?'"[116] (emphasis added)

While God may, sometimes, give a challenging word, correction, or strong conviction, whatever we share should build up, encourage, and comfort the person. If you sense God giving you something that will not build up, encourage, or comfort someone, it is important to run that insight by other people whom you trust so that you can seek Jesus for further guidance. If a word is directed to your church, it is important to submit it to the church leadership before blurting it out publicly.

Graham Cooke offers the following critical insight: "Revelatory prophecy, especially if it includes correction or direction, needs to have prior approval of leaders of the church, because whatever we hear from the Lord needs to be confirmed through the whole body of Christ. Prophets cannot give revelatory words with the same freedom and innocence as they do inspirational words."[117]

One Sunday evening, as the Tierra Nueva faith community stood in a circle for our weekly celebration of communion, a woman who was a regular visitor and had previously shared encouraging personal words with people, including one of our pastors, began to shout, "God is calling his people to repent of their sins!"

As she yelled this over and over, several people near her became agitated and confused. The Tierra Nueva community has many people in recovery, and some struggle with various degrees of mental health. I could see that her behavior was triggering some of these people, and others were moving away from her as if she were having a mental breakdown.

I walked over to her and quietly asked her to be at peace. I quoted Paul's words to the Corinthians: "God is not a God of confusion but of peace" (1 Cor 14:33). The woman told me that when the Spirit comes on her strongly, she loses control and must speak. I told her that Paul describes an order for gatherings, particularly prophecies, and that "the spirits of the prophets are subject to the prophets" (1 Cor 14:32). I explained that I thought Paul was saying that when God speaks to us, we have control over *what* we say, *when* we say it, and *how* we say it.

While God does call his people to repent of their sins, a true word from God's heart doesn't require shouting or dramatics, which can cause many people to feel distressed and confused. For a quiet word, full of the power of the Spirit, is perfectly capable of bringing about God's work. Unfortunately, some people (including the woman who visited Tierra Nueva that Sunday evening) may not be willing to receive this wise guidance from Scripture.

Humility

When a message that is supposed to be from God is delivered in way that is caustic or alienating, people tend to turn away rather than opening themselves to receive that word as a gift from God. So it is important for us to operate from a place of humility, acknowledging that we will get it wrong sometimes. This caution should guide *how* we share and *what* we share as a word from God's heart.

At Tierra Nueva, we have learned to avoid strong language, such as, "thus says the Lord," or, "Jesus is saying this right now." Instead, we offer what we are hearing more cautiously, as we have found it more effective to say, "As I pray, this thought is coming to me. Does that mean anything to you?" Or, "I have a sense that God is saying . . . Does this connect with you?" As Paul reminds us, we should test or examine all prophecies, *holding* to what is good and *abstaining* from anything that is not (1 Thess 5:20–21). This process of discernment applies to *what* we share as well as *how* we share it.

As I was praying about one of our ministry projects during a season when we did not have a leader, I thought of someone who might be good in that role. I emailed the person, saying that I had been praying about this project and her name had come to mind. Then I asked what she thought about leading that project. I thought this was a good, cautious way to mention a possible invitation from God, but the person I wrote felt that my message was manipulative, because I had framed it in the context of hearing from God in prayer. She felt that I was saying that *God* was telling her to take leadership over this project, which put pressure on her to say yes. Though we worked through this miscommunication, it taught me the importance of *how* we share and *what* we share about the things we hear as we listen to God's heart for others.

REVELATION, INTERPRETATION, APPLICATION

Whenever God shares his heart with us, it is always an invitation into an ongoing conversation. We may need to go much deeper in our listening before we can hear clearly. The three main layers we need to work through include *revelation, interpretation,* and *application.* We see this outlined in Paul's first letter to the Corinthians:

> What no eye has seen, nor ear heard, nor the heart of human-
> ity imagined, what God has prepared for those who love him—
> *these things God has revealed to us by the Spirit.* . . . Now we have
> received not the spirit of the world, but the Spirit who is from
> God, *that we might understand the things freely given us by God.*
> And we impart this in words not taught by human wisdom but
> taught by the Spirit, *interpreting spiritual truths* to those who are
> spiritual. (1 Cor 2:9–10, 12–13, emphasis added)

This passage highlights our connection to *God's Spirit,* not some disembodied source of power. When we pray, we are interacting with our living friend, Jesus, who invites us into an ongoing *conversation* with him. Thus we will need to dig deeper to discern what he is saying to us.

As Graham Cooke observes, "God wants us to explore and discover His diversity and the different ways in which we perceive and relate to Him… He is deliberately vague so that He can entice us into exploration and discovery. He is always bigger than our experience of Him."[118]

The first layer of exploration, *revelation,* refers to what the Holy Spirit is *revealing* from God's heart. This is our first awareness of what God is sharing with us—a word, image, feeling, vision, dream, or sense we have about something. This first layer of revelation marks the beginning of the conversation.

After we receive a revelation from the heart of God, we move into the second layer of exploration and discovery, which is *interpretation.* When we receive something from God, we might know who it's for, but we don't know what it means. In my desire to get things right or be thought of as spiritual and wise, I sometimes try to assign a meaning right away, but I must continually resist this temptation. As Paul notes, "we impart this in words not taught by human wisdom but taught by the Spirit, interpreting spiritual truths . . ." (1 Cor 2:13). Before assigning my limited human understanding to any word, I must first ask the Spirit, "What does this mean? Teach me how to interpret this spiritual truth."

This brings us to our third layer of exploration, *application,* which concerns *how* we are to respond to the revelation we have received. To discern how to apply what we think we have heard, we need to stay in communication with Jesus, asking, "What am I to do with this?" After God reveals what he is saying and helps us to understand what it means, our next step is to discern God's purpose. God may be giving us a word of encouragement or comfort to build us up so that it will be implanted in our hearts. Our response is simply to *trust* that what God is speaking to us is true. We may need to meditate on the word so that, over time, it will produce the fruit God intends. Or we may need to renounce certain lies that we have believed, which are contrary to this truth that God has revealed. Or God might be showing us something that will require repentance on our part. Or God may be inviting us to step out in faith in some way.

GOD DOESN'T MEASURE

While I was part of a prayer team at a conference in North Carolina, participants were invited to sign up to receive prayer for inner healing, physical healing, and prophetic encouragement from the Lord. Each prayer team listened to the person who was asking for prayer, then listened to the Holy Spirit, and then shared the words or read the Scriptures that God put on our hearts.

One pastor who approached our prayer team for prayer seemed heavy and depressed. As I looked at him, I had a vague impression about baseball. I didn't know what this sense at the edge of my perception meant, and so I ventured, "Do you play baseball?"

"No," he replied.

"Do you like baseball?" I asked.

"Not really."

I worried that I hadn't received this sense from God, and so I shared with this man that I didn't know why, but I found myself thinking about baseball as I looked at him.

I paused, and then I reflected about how baseball statistics are unlike any other sport. "I may be getting this wrong," I said, "but I think that a great batting average is around .300, and a .400 is nearly unachievable.

That means someone who hits the ball less than 30 percent of the time is considered a good hitter. In any other sport or job, if you only do what you are supposed to do 30 percent of the time, you'd be replaced by someone else!"

Then I sensed the Holy Spirit interpreting for me, and I said, "I wonder if you have a way of measuring yourself, and if God wants you to know that it's not the way he measures you. Just like baseball, what would appear poor by some measurement standards is exceptional in the kingdom. I wonder if God wants you to know that he doesn't measure you the way you measure yourself—or the way the world measures you. He delights in you. He says, 'You are a beloved son.' And, 'Well done, good and faithful one.'"

As I shared, this man began to cry. God had led me through a process so that I could understand more fully what was on his heart, but the revelation didn't come all at once. I had to keep listening to be able to move into interpretation and application.

God will often do interpretation and application through other people involved as part of God's ALL PLAY, so that we don't always look to one person, who seems to have all the gifts! For the gifts of the Holy Spirit are shared around the whole Body, so that each of us can play a part to build up, encourage, and comfort others with God's love—and each of us can be built up, encouraged, and comforted by that love.

TIMING

How God's word is revealed, interpreted, and applied is also affected by timing. While we may hear a word from God, it may not be for "now." In Isaiah 55:10–11, we see a picture of this:

> For as the rain and the snow come down from heaven and do not return there but water the earth, making it bring forth and sprout, giving seed to the sower and bread to the eater, *so shall my word be that goes out from my mouth; it shall not return to me empty but it shall accomplish that which I purpose, and shall succeed in the thing for which I send it.* (emphasis added)

God's word is compared to both the rain and the snow that water the ground. While the rain immediately seeps into the soil and goes to the roots, the snow builds up in the mountains during the winter and melts slowly, providing water to the rivers and streams during the summer months, when there is no rain. Rain provides water *now*, and snow provides water for a *later time*. Here in the Pacific Northwest, what falls as snow today in the mountains won't water our ground for several months, or sometimes years.

Similarly, when God shares his heart with us, he sometimes shares something for *right now* (like rain), but other times he shares something that is for a *later time* (like snow). When we receive a revelation, we may need to ask, "Is this a *now* word? Or is this *for a later time*?" If it is not for now, we need to ask *why* it is being revealed now. And we need to ask God what he wants us to do with it for the time being. Sometimes, rather than sharing what we are hearing from God, we need to store it and hold on to it, just as Mary, the mother of Jesus, did when the shepherds shared from God's heart about her son: for she "treasured up all these things, pondering them in her heart" (Luke 2:19).

As Graham Cooke confirms: "Some prophetic seasons must be spent praying before the throne over the prophetic input you have received. To pray in a prophetic word rather than speak it out is just as valid, powerful, and anointed."[119]

DISCERNMENT

This dynamic of divine–human cooperation in hearing and sharing what is on God's heart for someone else sets prophecy apart from fortune telling. When we receive a prophetic word, it is an invitation into deeper conversation with God. Before we risk sharing what is on God's heart, we need to pray and discern *what* to say, *how* to say it, and *when* to share it. We will discuss this process of discernment more in chapter 11, "Discerning God's Heart," but in concluding this chapter, I want to share the following key rule of discernment: *A prophetic word is not the end of the conversation with Jesus. It is the beginning.*

When we hear from God, we should not think, "God said it, and that settles it." Nor should we think, "Mike said this was a word from God, and that settles it." *Any* prophetic word is an invitation for the person who receives it to enter further into conversation with Jesus.

We might pray, "Jesus, Mike said this was from you. Can you confirm that for me? If it is from you, show me what it means? What should I do with it?" Even if a word comes from someone who appears to consistently hear from God, the word is still just the beginning of the conversation. As Paul reminds the church at Thessalonica, "test everything; hold fast to what is good" (1 Thess 5:21).

In our closing activation, we'll practice engaging in a discerning conversation with Jesus.

ACTIVATION

Take a moment to pause and be still. Breathe slowly. Focusing on your breath prayer, invite Jesus to be present. As you continue to breathe, invite Jesus to reveal his presence to you.

> *Holy Spirit, I invite you to bring someone to my mind whom you want to bless.*

Breathe and remain still until a face or name comes to mind.

> *Jesus, I invite you to share what is on your heart for _____?*
> *What do you want _____ to know?*

Pay careful attention to any thoughts that come to you—a name, face, Scripture, image, word, phrase, feeling, or sense. As these thoughts come, write them all down. Then pick one or two that strike you and enter into a conversation with Jesus.

As you talk with Jesus, invite the Spirit to reveal *what* of this word to share, *how* to share it, and *when* to share it.

As the Spirit prompts you, risk reaching out to this person to share what God has confirmed, following the guidelines outlined in this chapter. Or, if you sense this word is for a later time, bring it before Christ's throne in prayer, trusting the Spirit to remind you to keep praying until it is time for this word to be spoken.

You can also do this exercise in a small group. As you listen on behalf of one person, be sure to follow the guidelines for healthy, humble sharing. It is important that it is a safe space. Give each other the permission to get it wrong. Give yourself the permission to get it wrong.

Chapter 11

DISCERNING GOD'S HEART

"All our experience is structured, and the structures we use are the products of our past experiences; we cannot have a "pure" experience unaffected by the structures of our own personalities and minds, themselves the products of living in a certain culture. How can we be sure that our "experiences of God" are really "of God" and not "of ourselves"?"

—William A. Barry and William J. Connelly,
The Practice of Spiritual Direction

THE VOICE OF THE GOOD SHEPHERD

One of the most common questions people ask when I talk about hearing God's voice is, "How do I know I am hearing God and not just myself?" This is a very important question. Jesus acknowledges the complexity of discerning what we hear when he compares the voice of the Good Shepherd with the voices of strangers:

> "Truly, truly I say to you, he who does not enter the sheepfold by the door, but climbs in by some other way, that man is a thief and a robber. But he who enters by the door is the shepherd of the sheep. To him the gatekeeper opens. The sheep hear his voice, and he calls his own sheep by name and leads them out. When he has brought out all his own, he goes before them, and the sheep

follow him because they know his voice. A stranger they will not follow, but they will flee from him, because they do not know the voice of strangers. . . . The thief comes only to steal and kill and destroy. I came that they may have life and have it abundantly." (John 10:1–5, 10)

Though Jesus strongly affirms that his sheep "hear his voice" and follow him because "they know his voice," he points out that there are other voices at play, for his sheep will not follow a stranger, "because they do not know the voice of strangers" (10:5). The other players he mentions include a robber who climbs over the wall (10:1), wolves that come to scatter (10:12), and a thief who comes to steal, kill, and destroy (10:10).

In this parable, Jesus is talking to his listeners about the nature of sheep, who come to associate the sound of the shepherd's voice with certain benefits. They know who feeds them, who protects them, and who cares for their needs. Sheep can distinguish their keeper's voice from others' voices because they have come to trust the shepherd, who is always talking to them. Because the sheep *know* his voice, they follow him. But sheep won't follow a stranger's voice, because they have not come to know or trust the stranger. Instead, the sheep will flee from the stranger (10:5).

In connecting this parable to our own hearing God's voice, we face a challenge, for we have spent a lot of time in places other than the pasture that is being tended by the Good Shepherd. As a result, we have many voices in our heads that are *not* the voice of Jesus, and yet we don't discern them as *strangers*, because we are all too familiar with them. These include the voices of shame and condemnation, fear and anxiety, anger, resentment, and pride. They include the voices we use to defend or promote ourselves. In fact, we have often followed these voices, and we already associate them with certain benefits. Though they are familiar, they have come like thieves and robbers to steal from us, to kill and destroy. Yet Jesus, the Good Shepherd, wants us to follow his voice so that he can lead us to a free and abundant life (10:10).

Identifying Competing Voices: the World and the Flesh

I encountered this challenge to know the voice of the Good Shepherd once when I prayed with a woman who was diagnosed with bipolar disorder. At the end of our time, she had a beautiful and significant encounter with Jesus in her imagination, and Jesus spoke things to her that she needed to hear. When she had finished meeting with Jesus, she opened her eyes and said, "You shouldn't tell crazy people to hear voices."

I smiled and told her, "You're not crazy—and I hear voices, too." Then I went on to explain that our challenge is to discern *which* voices should have our attention.

We may start our life with God by surrendering to Jesus, but we are often unaware of the radical countercultural call of his kingdom and its values that are to be part of our ongoing discipleship and being transformed more into the likeness of Jesus. Without this transforming work, we can end up simply adding Jesus onto all the other "kingdoms of this world" values which are all things we have grown up believing, thereby baptizing many "non-Jesus" ways of thinking with a Christian veneer. These "worldly" values and ways of thinking come from our family systems, cultures, experiences, and even church cultures, and all these competing voices can color what we believe we "hear" when we listen to the heart of God.

Along with all these voices from the world, we run up against what the Bible calls "the flesh." In Paul's letter to the Galatians, he tells us that "the desires of the flesh are against the Spirit and the desires of the Spirit are against the flesh" (Gal 5:17). While I've heard the "flesh" generally defined as our sin nature and our propensity to sin, I have come to think of the flesh as all the ways we have learned to survive apart from trusting in Jesus. The flesh includes all our coping strategies, defense mechanisms, addictions, *and* sinful behaviors. And the flesh includes all the ways we seek to have our needs for security, significance, and acceptance met rather than receiving them from God. Many, including psychologist David Benner describe this as *the false self*, when he says, "Everything that is false about us rises from our belief that our deepest happiness will come from living life our way, not God's way."[120] This belief is so deeply ingrained in us that we often live from this self without being aware that we are listening to so many competing voices in our heads.

In Paul's letter to the Ephesians, he writes that those who follow Christ are to "put off [our] old self which belongs to [our] former manner of life and is corrupt through deceitful desires, and to be renewed in the spirit of [our] minds, and to put on the new self, created after the likeness of God in true righteousness and holiness" (Eph 4:22–24).

Paul's description of "putting on" a "new self" reminds me of my friend, Mark, who left a life of atheism and incarceration to follow Jesus. As Mark sought to "put off" his old life, he found that he had to call into question *every* single thought, belief, decision, value, and action he had ever had. But as he sought to "put on" his new self in Christ, he realized that God's voice was the only quiet voice in his head, and he could trust that he was hearing from God when whatever he heard was the *opposite* of what came naturally to him.

This highlights the importance of becoming more self-aware so that we can distinguish God's voice from all the opposing voices within us. We have already explored how our experiences of pain, shame, brokenness, and sin can distort what we hear from God.[121] We have also discussed how our toxic theologies and political, economic, racial, and other worldly ideologies have given us false or incomplete images of God, which do not reflect what Jesus reveals about the Father.

IDENTIFYING THE VOICE OF THE ENEMY

Now we will turn to the Gospels, which can help reveal our incomplete images of God in contrast to how Jesus talks about his Father.

In Matthew 16, Jesus is traveling with his disciples, and he asks them a core question about his identity: "Who do you say that I am?"

> Simon Peter replied, "You are the Christ, the Son of the living God." And Jesus answered him, "Blessed are you, Simon son of Jonah! For flesh and blood did not reveal this to you, but my Father who is in heaven . . . " (Matt 16:16–17)

In other words, Peter has received a revelation from the Father about Jesus. We all long for such a beautiful and powerful encounter with God! A few verses later, Jesus gives the interpretation of Peter's revelation, explaining that being Messiah will involve betrayal, suffering, and death at the hands of religious and political leaders—and then resurrection. Then, as Matthew describes it:

> Peter took [Jesus] aside and began to rebuke him, saying, "Far be it from you, Lord! This shall never happen to you!" But [Jesus] turned and said to Peter, "Get behind me, Satan! You are a hindrance to me. For you are not setting your mind on the things of God, but on the things of man." (Matt 16:22–23)

Having heard directly from God about the identity of Jesus, Peter may be feeling confident that he is more dialed in than the other disciples. Then he takes the revelation from God about Jesus and puts a cultural, political, and religious filter on it so that he can *interpret* what the revelation *means*. Peter's historical, national, and religious culture already had very strong ideas about who the Messiah would be and what he would do: a victorious military leader kicking the Romans out of Israel and making God's people great again! This victorious Messiah most certainly would not suffer and be killed by the Romans, for the Messiah would reestablish Israel as the greatest of all earthly kingdoms (cf. Acts 1:6).

Yet Jesus rebukes Peter and identifies the source of his interpretation as Satan! How can Peter receive a massive revelation from the Father in heaven one minute—and in the very next minute, receive an interpretation from hell? How can Satan be identified as the source of this new revelation? Is Peter practicing witchcraft? Jesus explains that Peter's mind is set *on the things of man.* In other words, his mind is set on his religious, cultural, political, and historical interpretation of God's promises—rather than the revelation of *God's heart in Jesus* and the scandal of a crucified Messiah (cf. 1 Cor 1:22).

It is easy to sit back and judge Peter for getting it so wrong. We can always see it in others! Yet we can each hear from both heaven and hell. We can each listen to God the Father and also the things of the world. Our beliefs about God and God's kingdom collide with our earthly values and our fleshly strategies, making it difficult to discern God's voice from all the other competing voices in our heads and distorting, especially, how we interpret what we hear. Like Peter, we can get the revelation really right—and we can get the interpretation really wrong.

CHARTING A PATH FOR OUR ONGOING DISCERNMENT

With so many competing voices, how can we know that what we are hearing is from God's heart—and not a stranger, the world, the flesh, or the enemy?

As I mentioned earlier in chapter 7, my friend Libby divides the work of discerning God's voice into three main buckets.[122] She explains that if you hear, "I love you," "I want to be with you," or "You are so dear to me," you can just receive that. And if you hear anything that shames, accuses, or tears you down, you can just throw that out—or at least set it aside to be processed later, "because something is warping what you are hearing." For everything in between, you "want to talk some more with Jesus and with others."[123]

In the next sections, we will explore several questions that can guide our discernment as we dialogue with Jesus and others about the things we place in the "middle" bucket, where we put "everything in between."

LISTENING TO THE VOICE OF JESUS: THE CENTER OF OUR DISCERNMENT

The writer of the Gospel of John says in his first epistle (written in his old age, long after Jesus had been crucified and resurrected):

> Dear friends, do not believe every spirit, but *test* the spirits to see whether they are from God, because many false prophets have gone out into the world. *This is how you can recognize the Spirit of God*: Every spirit that acknowledges that Jesus Christ has come in the flesh *is* from God, but every spirit that does not acknowledge Jesus *is not* from God. (1 John 4:1–3, emphasis added)

My friend Chris Walker, in his teaching on how to discern the work of the Holy Spirit, says it like this: "The Holy Spirit has a single-minded focus on Jesus Christ as the truth and will bring glory to Jesus alone."[124]

This points to our first discernment question, which is:

Does what we are hearing point us toward Jesus and give him glory?

This is an important question, but we may not know immediately if a word we hear gives glory to Jesus, or not. If we don't know, we can ask further questions, such as, "Does what I am hearing lead me to greater dependence on Jesus?" If it leads us toward selfishness, dishonesty, or trusting in our own abilities, we know that we are *not* hearing the voice of the Good Shepherd.

When people talk about discerning the voice of God, they often ask, "Is what I am hearing consistent with the *Bible*?" Unfortunately, throughout history we have justified all kinds of atrocities through Scripture— including genocide, slavery, systems of supremacy and control, racism, the subjugation of women, the Crusades, many wars, and so on. So this question is too general. Others might ask, "Is what I am hearing consistent with the *character of God* revealed in the Bible." But people can claim to speak for God and then declare terrible things based on violent interpretations of the Old Testament that contradict the heart of God, which is revealed in Jesus alone.[125]

Because Jesus alone came to reveal the heart of his Father, our primary tool for discerning the voice of the Good Shepherd must be the Good Shepherd himself. So our second question focuses our gaze specifically on Jesus:

Is what we are hearing consistent with the character of God as revealed in Jesus?

In other words, does it look like Jesus, sound like Jesus, and feel like the Jesus of the Gospels? As Rich Villodas, who is the pastor of a multi-ethnic parish in Queens (with more than seventy-five countries represented), observes, "Christians can read the Bible every day and still have our hearts firmly against the ways of the Kingdom of God. Unless we read scripture through the lens of the crucified Christ, with others, our exegesis is dangerously subject to personal preferences and political allegiances."[126]

The Jesus of the Gospels reveals that "God is for us and not against us" (Rom 8:31). And Jesus is called the "Friend of sinners" (Matt 11:19) as throughout the Gospels, he eats meals with "sinners" and calls tax collectors and zealots—and even those who end up betraying him—to follow him.[127] Jesus breaks religious rules to heal and free those who are considered outcasts and cursed by God.[128] Jesus flips the tables on what it looks like to be blessed in the Beatitudes (Matt 5:3-12). And in the parable of the prodigal son, Jesus reveals to us the loving and forgiving heart of God, the Father (Luke 15:11–32). When God speaks to us through his son, the Good Shepherd, it will sound like the voice of Jesus.

My friend, Chris Hoke, often challenged my images of God saying, "If it sounds too good to be true, it's probably Jesus." While this quip may not be a sharp enough tool for our discernment, it can help us reorient our reference point to the Jesus of the Gospels, who is full of grace, truth, and compassion—particularly if our previous filters included images of an angry, punitive, or disappointed God. That mad and disappointed voice is the *accuser of the brothers and sisters* from the book of Revelation (12:10), who judges and condemns us day and night, the one whom Jesus describes as the thief who comes to steal, kill, and destroy (John 10:10).

And yet, discernment is so important here because while Jesus *is* better than we've been told, he may have hard things to say to us. He is full of grace *and truth*. We see this in the gospels especially toward religious leaders and, at times, with his disciples. Love may need to get in our face and call out all that is opposed to that Love. Henri Nouwen acknowledges this challenge when he says, "Yes, God is a demanding God, God's love is a persistent love, and when God demands a lot from us, it is out of divine love."[129]

Sometimes it is hard for us to see our way through the quagmire of our competing images of God. We can think of these as *blind spots* precisely because we can't *see* them. This leads us to the importance of tuning our hearts to the love of God so that we will be able to discern the filters that can distort God's voice.

I've read that bank tellers learn to identify counterfeit money, not by examining all the various types of counterfeit bills, but by handling the true currency over and over, so that when the false comes along, they can sense that something is off. The Jesus of the Gospels is our true currency. The more time we spend with him, the more aware we will be when we are hearing something counterfeit.

LISTENING TO THE HOLY SPIRIT

In Romans 8:16, Paul tells us that "the Spirit himself bears witness with our spirit that we are children of God." When God *bears witness with our spirit*, we sense an inner *yes* as our spirit *resonates* with what the Holy Spirit is saying. This leads to our third question:

> *Does the Holy Spirit testify to our heart that what we are hearing is the truth?*

My friend Aaron White, who lives and ministers in the Downtown Eastside (DTES) neighborhood of Vancouver, British Columbia,[130] did a teaching on prophecy. After someone asked, "How can you know if it is God speaking?" someone else replied, "I like to flip the question. *How do you know the voice of a loved one is speaking to you?* How would you describe that?"[131]

Our inner *yes* is connected to a relationship of love. We have come to know the voice of the Good Shepherd, who loves us and cares for us. Jesus encourages us, "My sheep know my voice."[132] We can listen to our heart when we sense, *yes, that is my Good Shepherd's voice.* Thus discernment is not so much about following a *formula*, but growing in *familiarity* with Jesus.

Even still, we might be afraid that we are *just* hearing *ourselves* speaking. Leanne Payne addresses this concern in *Listening Prayer*: "Although there is a validity to that particular caution . . . when we are one with Christ, why are we afraid to know what 'just me' knows—what our hearts from their depths can speak? Within a short time you will be able to discern the difference between . . . the wisdom already given you and the word God speaks to you afresh. Both are important and needful."[133]

DISCERNING OUR IDOLS

Yet Scripture cautions us against trusting our hearts, which Payne acknowledges when she says there is "validity to that particular caution." Our inner voice can become clouded, and so true heart discernment will involve sifting through our *idols*. The prophet Ezekiel describes this process as follows:

> Then some elders of Israel came to me and sat down before me. And the word of the Lord came to me, saying, "Son of man, these men have set up their idols in their hearts and have put in front of their faces the stumbling block of their wrongdoing. Should I let Myself be consulted by them at all? Therefore, speak to them and tell them, 'This is what the Lord God says: "Anyone of the house of Israel *who sets up his idols in his heart*, puts in front of his face the stumbling block of his wrongdoing, and then comes to the prophet, I the Lord will let Myself answer him in the matter in view of the multitude of his idols . . ." (Ezekiel 14:1–4, emphasis added)

We all have idols in our hearts—things we look to other than God for our sense of security, significance, or acceptance, and for power, control, or survival. Our idols can include relationships, the validation of others, money, power, politics, race, sex, safety, provision, and all our fears around these things. Tim Keller, chairman and co-founder Redeemer City to City, notes that "An idol is whatever you look at and say, in your heart of hearts, 'If I have that thing, then I'll feel my life has meaning, then I'll know I have value, then I'll feel significant and secure."[134]

We run after idols and serve them, investing time, energy, and money to obtain them, and then we fight for them and make sacrifices to hold onto them. Wherever we may be on the political spectrum, we all fight for certain *individual* rights. And one way we can identify an idol is by the way we react when that right is threatened or overturned. Jesus said that we can't love both God and money (Luke 16:13)—and our ongoing attempts to explain away this statement is a good indicator that he is exposing this as an idol!

Idols can make it difficult for us to discern God's heart, because we start to look to them to tell us what is true about the world, ourselves, and *about God*. When we believe in our hearts that certain things are valuable, important, and right, we can begin to believe that God feels the same way as we do—that God approves of our values, politics, economics, and culture.

Bob Ekblad identifies an idol as anything we put in the place of the Father, whatever we trust to "call the shots." We often baptize these idols as "Christian," creating God as an image of our own needs and desires, our culture and nation. As Tim Keller puts it, "If God never disagrees with you, you might be worshipping an idealized version of yourself."[135] That would be an idol!

God tells Ezekiel (14:1–9) that the leaders have taken idols into their hearts, which impacts what they believe they are hearing from God. The Lord says that when people with such idols come to inquire of the Lord, the answer they will receive will be *according to their idolatry* (v. 4). In other words, the person seeking a word from God will hear a reflection of the idolatry in their hearts rather than a word of truth from the heart of God.

DISCERNING WITH OTHERS

My inner idols highlight my need to be listening to and discerning the heart of God in community by asking people we trust if what we are hearing sounds like Jesus. As Leann Payne cautions us: "If we are not listening to God together with God's people, we endanger our private listening. . . . Our brothers and sisters are gifted by the Spirit in ways we are not. Their speaking and listening to God sharpens ours, adding dimensions of wisdom and knowledge we would not gain otherwise."[136] This insight points toward our fourth discernment question:

> *What do people we trust to hear God's heart have to say about what we are hearing?*

God created us to depend on one another and to work together for his kingdom. As Paul writes in his first letter to the Corinthians: "we know *in part*, and we prophesy *in part*" (1 Cor 13:9, emphasis added). God shares the gifts of the Holy Spirit with the whole body so that no one will receive *all* the gifts or the *same* gifts, and we will need each other. Paul instructs the church at Corinth to: "Let two or three prophets speak, and let others weigh what is said" (1 Cor 14:29). In this way, the community relies on each other to build up the whole *body* of Christ. Listening for God's voice is healthiest when it happens in community—not simply on our own.

I meet regularly with several men to talk about what God is doing in our lives. As we listen to each other and to the Spirit, we ask one another questions that help clarify what God may be saying. Recently, my friend asked me what I felt God was saying, and I shared that I felt God was challenging me to create more space to be still and listen to him. After a brief silence, my friend wondered if I was being too hard on myself. Then he named all the ways I was already making space and reflected that whatever God was saying, he didn't think it was about *working* harder.

Later, I reflected in my journal:

> *I felt the word, "you are being too hard on yourself," very deeply as a grace and gift—the word of Jesus to me. I am often hard on myself for not measuring up to some standard. I've always got to be working on something or performing better, doing more to receive what God has, become more disciplined. I sense this word also extends to my work and relationships, all the places where I don't feel I am enough and need to try harder.*

Performance is still a deeply rooted filter in me, and though I am more aware of how it works in me, I continue to need people whom I trust to help me discern what God might be saying to me.

DISCERNING OUR FRUIT: BECOMING LIKE JESUS

Having talked about the *inner yes* and the reality that we can have a lot of inner blind spots, we also need to acknowledge that our listening community has its own cultural and theological blind spots, especially if our community is homogenous, made up of people who are mostly like us. It is so easy to listen to God's voice within socio-economic, racial, and cultural bubbles. We've already asked if what we are hearing looks, sounds, and feels like Jesus. We also need to ask if what we are hearing moves us to *become* more like Jesus or less. After checking the *inner yes* of our hearts, we also need to check the *outer yes* of our community by asking this fifth discernment question:

Will it make us more or less like Jesus?

As we give God our attention and gaze on the crucified and risen Jesus, God will slowly transform us into the image of Jesus. Paul describes this as follows: "we all, with unveiled face, beholding the glory of the Lord, are being *transformed into the same image* from one degree of glory to another. This comes from the Lord, who is the Spirit" (2 Cor 3:18, emphasis added).

We can frame that discernment question a bit differently by asking,

How will what we are hearing transform us into the image of Christ?

Such transformation involves growth and change, which is often difficult and painful. The author of Hebrews tells us that Jesus, himself, was perfected by suffering,[137] and Paul tells us we are to have the same mind that is in Christ Jesus who became obedient to death on a cross.[138] The image of Jesus we gaze upon is the crucified Savior. Even the risen Jesus is portrayed as the Lamb who was slain.[139] There is much we miss of the heart of God until we are in a place of struggle. As we grow in greater dependence upon God, God's love will call us to face our fears and lead us out of our comfort zones, helping us learn how to endure hard things "with patience and joy" (Col 1:11). This may involve "sharing in the fellowship of his sufferings" (Phil 3:10), because the goal is for us to "grow up in every way into him who is the Head, into Christ" (Eph 4:15). The Holy Spirit is committed to our transformation, and struggle and suffering are often the primary crucible that makes us more like Jesus.

Finally, Jesus warned that we would know false prophets by their *fruit* (Matt 7:15–17). So our last discernment question is:

What kind of fruit will this produce in our lives?

This question includes the impact that what we are hearing will have on others in the community. In fine-tuning this question, we might ask if what we are sensing will produce the fruit of the Spirit—love, joy, peace, patience, kindness, goodness, gentleness, faithfulness, and self-control—in us and our community. The book of James adds: "But the wisdom that comes from heaven is first of all pure; then peace-loving, considerate, submissive, full of mercy and good fruit, impartial and sincere" (Jas 3:18). If we see evidence of these things, we can trust that what we are hearing will produce *good fruit* in us and our community.

DISCERNMENT AT WORK

As we seek to hear what is on God's heart, it is important to have many points of discernment, because we can get it right in one area and be completely off in others. Peter got the revelation that Jesus was "Messiah, Son of God" right, but he got the interpretation of what that meant completely wrong, because he filtered it through the religious, Judeo-nationalist filter of his time. What we hear might sound to us like Jesus, but we may have a skewed idea of what Jesus is like! Or we may sense an inner *yes* but be filled with distorting filters and idolatries. We may open ourselves to listen with others, but our community may be operating in an echo chamber with its own blind spots.

As we grow in discernment within our communities, we will need to keep surrendering our ideologies and idolatries, discerning what is from the worldly empire and what is truly of the kingdom of God, by asking the Holy Spirit to reveal our blind spots and distorting filters.

To help establish a concrete context for the discernment process I've outlined in this chapter, I have taken a "test case" from my own life regarding a communication that I received from God.

Most of the things I hear when I engage in daily conversations with Jesus and interact with Scripture are words of encouragement and comfort or challenges for my own growth, which I don't run through the discernment questions I outlined above. But the words I have received that feel bigger, or that are about life changes definitely go into a "middle bucket," which I set aside for further conversation with God and others.

Remember that the most important rule of discernment is that any word from Jesus is not the end of the conversation, but the *beginning*. In the following test case, I'll run what I heard through each of the six discernment questions mentioned above.

A TEST CASE FOR DISCERNMENT

As I was sitting at our kitchen table reading one winter afternoon, a thought came to me "out of nowhere," completely disconnected from anything I had been thinking, reading, or praying about. The thought, which came clearly and insistently, was that it was time for me to move from my work at Tierra Nueva into an independent prayer, teaching, and mentoring ministry connected to spiritual direction.

I suspected this "out of nowhere" thought was from the Holy Spirit, as this has become a *familiar* aspect of God's communication over the past several years. Yet this thought was connected to a big life change, and so I put it in my bucket for further conversation with God and others.

Does what I am hearing point me toward Jesus and give him glory?

As I reflected on this question, I considered how this new vocation might point toward Jesus and give him glory *more* than faithfully continuing my work with Tierra Nueva. I noted that the change would certainly lead me into greater dependence on Jesus, because I don't like change—I like stability. Leaving my work at Tierra Nueva after thirteen years would require me to trust I was truly hearing Jesus speak. To follow this word, I would have to keep my eyes constantly fixed on Jesus to see what he was doing. I felt a strong conviction that this was his idea, not mine. So I moved to the second question.

Is what I am hearing consistent with the character of God as revealed in Jesus?

I took a moment to reflect on Jesus as he is depicted in the Gospels. I noticed him calling Simon and his brother Andrew to leave the net they were casting into the sea and follow him (Matt 4:18–20). And then I saw him calling James and John to leave the net they were mending with their father to follow him (Matt 4:21–22). I noticed him calling Levi to leave his work as a tax collector and step out in faith to follow him (Mark 2:14). As I watched Jesus calling his disciples in the Gospels, I sensed that he might be calling me into a new place of trust and dependence on him as well. But I also sensed that I could continue to love and serve Jesus by staying and continuing to follow him in my work at Tierra Nueva.

As I stepped back to consider the bigger picture, I felt the Spirit guiding me to look over my journals from the previous year or so. As I began to read over these words, visions and dreams which I had sensed were from God but didn't know how to interpret them at the time, I found a common thread connecting them to one another and to this most recent word about a season of transition.

This connection led me to the third discernment question.

Does the Holy Spirit testify to my heart that what I am hearing is the truth?

As I began to make connections between so many seemingly disconnected words over the previous years, my inner *yes* resonated more strongly. At the same time, stepping into change does not come naturally to me, and so I was aware that I was moving out of my comfort zone. This was not what came naturally to me.

I had never thought seriously about spiritual direction, though I had vaguely thought of pursuing training in this area. But the fact that this thought had come to me "out of nowhere" suggested that I was not making it up on my own. This made my inner *yes* resonate even more strongly.

What do people I trust to hear God's heart have to say about what I am hearing?

Later, as I reflected on this word with Susan, she reminded me that I am not a dreamer by nature, and yet she could see that I was *dreaming with God* about this new venture. As I brought this thought to people who supported my work at Tierra Nueva, they all encouraged me and confirmed the direction that I sensed Jesus calling me as well as my particular gifts for this new work.

Then I received a particularly compelling confirmation from our friend, Rita, whom I trust to hear from God. After sharing what I sensed I was hearing, she smiled and then said, "Jesus already told me all that."

Surprised, I asked, "What did Jesus tell you?"

"He said, 'I've invited Mike to leave Tierra Nueva and do spiritual direction.'"

With that final confirmation, I felt peace to move forward with the process of leaving Tierra Nueva and step into this new spiritual direction ministry. Over the course of that transition, I have made space to reflect on the final two discernment questions.

Will it make me more or less like Jesus?

Between stepping out of my role at Tierra Nueva and starting Emmaus Road Ministries Northwest, the months of transition were marked by deeper surrender to Jesus and a greater awareness of the areas in my life that I have still not surrendered. Throughout this season, I wrestled with my sense of identity being attached to what I do and how I think people perceive me. This season also revealed more of my brokenness as well as more of my belovedness. In this, I have sensed God tilling the soil of my soul and drawing me into deeper intimacy with Jesus.

What kind of fruit will this produce in my life?

Because we often need others to help us see the slow-growing fruit in our lives, I asked Susan if she could identify any fruit that this season has brought about in my life. She observed that she has seen me become freer and less burdened as I have spent time dreaming with God. She also senses us moving into more of a partnership. We both think this is good fruit!

ACTIVATION

Take a moment to practice discerning something that you sense you have heard from God. You might read through your journal and find one of the exercises from a previous chapter, where you have encountered Jesus or received a communication from God's heart. In this exercise, you are looking for something from the "middle bucket," which requires further conversation with God and others.

As you reflect on this word that you sense God has spoken to you, consider each of the following discernment questions and respond to them in your journal and in conversation with others.

Does what you are hearing point toward Jesus and give Him glory?

Is what you are hearing consistent with the character of God as revealed in Jesus?

Does the Holy Spirit testify to your heart that what you are hearing is the truth?

What do people you trust to hear God's heart have to say about what you are hearing?

Will this make you more like Jesus? What kind of fruit will this produce in your life?

Chapter 12

HEARING GOD'S HEART FOR THE WORLD: PROPHETIC JUSTICE

"Is not this the kind of fasting I have chosen:
to loose the chains of injustice and untie the cords of the yoke,
to set the oppressed free and break every yoke?
Is it not to share your food with the hungry
and to provide the poor wanderer with shelter—
when you see the naked, to clothe them
and not to turn away from your own flesh and blood?"

—Isaiah 58:6–7

Several years ago, during the second Obama administration, I was speaking at a conference on the Holy Spirit, and I shared about what God was doing in my work among those who have been impacted by immigration, incarceration, and addiction with Tierra Nueva. Following my teaching, I was approached by an older man who was offended by my reference to social justice as part of the work of the Holy Spirit. He felt that the term, "social justice," was part of the progressive partisan agenda and therefore had no place in teaching from the Bible. This interaction highlights how when we talk about the Holy Spirit and hearing God's heart, we can focus on the *personal prophetic*, or the gift of prophecy, and miss the *social prophetic*, which includes the call to speak and work for God's heart for justice.

As we seek to listen to God's heart for the world, we don't have to read very far in the Bible before we run into God's particular concern for the poor, oppressed, fatherless, widow, alien, stranger, and the excluded—those who, as theologian Howard Thurman puts it, "stand with their backs against the wall."[140] God's *predisposition* for the poor is engraved in the Law and ratified in the prophets.[141]

We often spiritualize the teaching and ministry of Jesus, as if his primary purpose was to get us saved and into heaven. But Jesus himself speaks in very concrete terms about what it looks like to establish his just kingdom on earth.

In *A Farewell to Mars: An Evangelical Pastor's Journey Toward the Biblical Gospel of Peace*, Brian Zahnd talks about the challenge of believing in Jesus when it comes to his political theology:

> Our personal experience with the Kingdom of God (including forgiveness) is our personal experience of salvation, but the Kingdom of God is much bigger than our personal experience of it. . . . Once you see that Jesus has his own political agenda, his own vision for arranging human society, his own criteria for judging nations, then it's impossible to give your heart to the power-based, win-at-all-costs partisan politics that call for our allegiance.[142]

We see this when Jesus outlines his prophetic criteria for the final judgment in Matthew 25, which appear to say nothing about praying a sinner's prayer so we can get into heaven:

> "Then he will say to those on his left, 'Depart from me, you cursed, into the eternal fire prepared for the devil and his angels. For I was hungry, and you gave me no food, I was thirsty and you gave me no drink, I was a stranger and you did not welcome me, naked and you did not clothe me, sick and in prison and you did not visit me.'
>
> "Then they also will answer, saying, 'Lord, when did we see you hungry or thirsty or a stranger or naked or sick or in prison, and did not minister to you?'

"Then he will answer them, saying, 'Truly, I say to you, as you did not do it to one of the least of these, you did not do it to me.'" (Matt 25:41–46)

In my own faith journey, I have so often glossed over or completely missed these portions of Scripture that lift up the oppressed because they don't speak directly to my place of personal struggle. Or I have avoided them because of my guilt and shame, and the fear of the cost.

When Jesus declares, "How difficult it is for those with wealth to enter the Kingdom of God,"[143] he is recognizing that many who seek to follow him have benefitted from the systems of the world that have oppressed others. Yet it is so easy for our familial and cultural filters to keep us from hearing what God is saying to us in the Bible—and has been saying all along—about justice and equity for *all*. When we encounter this costly call to following the way of Jesus, we may be tempted to close our ears and harden our hearts so that we don't have to hear what is on God's heart.

MY JOURNEY INTO GOD'S HEART FOR JUSTICE

Prior to that conference, in 2007, when I learned that my associate pastor position at a mainstream Presbyterian church in Seattle was being downsized, several friends suggest that I connect with Bob Ekblad because he was exploring the intersection of social justice and the empowering work of the Holy Spirit. So on a rainy Wednesday afternoon, I drove north to Burlington, where Bob and his wife, Gracie, shared their journey beginning with their work among the poor *campesinos* in the mountainous region of central Honduras in the early 1980s to Washington State in 1994, where they started Tierra Nueva del Norte ("New Earth of the North"), a ministry among the migrant farmworker community, and Bob became a chaplain in the Skagit County jail. As Bob and Gracie accompanied people through oppressive systems and addictions, they told me that they became completely overwhelmed by the need and cried out to God, "Is there a gospel that has the power to *save*?" Teetering on the edge of burnout, they wondered if there was a gospel that would make a difference in *this* life and not just the next.

As they continue to cry out to God for a gospel that could *save* the addicts and inmates they were accompanying through Tierra Nueva, Bob and Gracie attended a conference at the Toronto Airport Christian Fellowship. At the end of one of the sessions, Bob waited in a line of people to receive prayer. A young man from England came to Bob and began to pray, then lightly touched his fingers to Bob's chest and said, "I see you in a room with blue plastic chairs and men in red jumpsuits," (an exact description of the room in the Skagit County Jail where Bob led Bible studies), "and I hear the Father say, 'I love how you love my prisoners.'"

Hearing "prophetically" that these inmates were seen and loved by God opened Bob's heart, and the young man continued that God would pour out his Holy Spirit with fresh power and give Bob fresh insight into the Scriptures that would make these beloved prisoners' hearts burn with prophetic words and healing. As Bob and Gracie remembered this encounter, they shared how this was the *good news* they had been seeking—a gospel that combined the prophetic power of the Holy Spirit with God's heart for social justice.

As I listened to their story, I recognized that I had spent so many years in dry obedience, not experiencing God's true heart for me or the goodness of God's presence. In the midst of my transition away from pastoring in a mainstream Presbyterian church, I felt thirsty for the outpouring of the Holy Spirit that I could see was empowering Bob and Gracie.

Sensing the invitation to come and see, my wife and I took a class taught by Bob titled "Exodus and Liberation," which he was offering through The Peoples Seminary of Tierra Nueva. As Bob guided our class through Exodus 1, he revealed how God aligns himself with the oppressed and most vulnerable rather than those in power (the Empire and its systems of oppression). He also highlighted how God blessed the Hebrew midwives for their resistance to the orders of the Empire, which instructed them to kill all the male Hebrew children. When it comes to the oppression of people, God is not a "law and order" God!

In Exodus 2, Bob drew our attention to the Hebrew word, *ra'ah*, which shows up often and can be translated as "to see." Throughout Exodus, the seeing implied by *ra'ah* leads to actions of resistance and liberation. For example, Moses's mother "*saw* he was a fine child, and she hid him for three months" (2:2). The daughter of Pharaoh "*saw* the basket among the reeds and . . . took it" (2:5). When she opened the basket, "she *saw* the child . . . and took pity on him" (2:6). Later, the young adult Moses "*saw* an Egyptian beating a Hebrew and . . . struck down the Egyptian" (2:11). And "God *saw* [the suffering of] the people of Israel—and God knew" (2:25).

This theme of *seeing* continues in Exodus 3. Out in the wilderness, while tending sheep, Moses *sees* the burning bush and says, "'I will turn aside and *see*'" (3:3). As Moses stops to *see* why the bush is burning, yet not consumed, he encounters God, who speaks to the concern has been burning in Moses' heart since he was a child: "The Lord said, 'I have surely *seen* the affliction of my people" (3:7), and "I have also *seen* the oppression with which the Egyptians oppress them" (3:9). As a result of all this *seeing*, God declares, "Therefore, come now, and I will send you to Pharaoh that you may bring my people, the children of Israel, out of Egypt" (3:10).

Seeing oppression and injustice is the first step to connecting with God's heart for prophetic justice (the social prophetic), which is a central concern of the Old Testament and also the ministry of Jesus. In this prophetic tradition, the chief role of the prophet is to *speak* the word of the Lord (the truth of God's heart) to those in power who are oppressing the poor and vulnerable.

Those of us who have grown up in mainstream church and society often skim over these passages in the Bible, or we tend to think of *ourselves* as the oppressed. Though we have all experienced suffering, hardship, and trauma—and God wants to meet us in those places and bring healing—the reality is that, for many of us, *our* place in the system has more in common with the Egyptians, who benefitted from the policies of Pharaoh, than the oppressed and marginalized Hebrews. But when we read the Bible solely for our personal devotions and in our cultural bubbles, it is very difficult to *see* this. Moses had to fall from his position of power and privilege before he could *see*. And I had to leave my mainstream, middle-class church and come to Tierra Nueva before I could begin to *see*.

In chapter 10, "Hearing God's Heart for Others: Partnership and Prophecy," we looked at three layers of prophetic exploration: *revelation, interpretation,* and *application.* Bob Ekblad identifies these layers with three actions: "*see, judge,* and *act.*" He says that this "structured approach to contextual Bible study . . . began in Latin America in the 1960s and has spread throughout the world, mostly in Roman Catholic communities."[144]

The act of *seeing* is the starting place, where God first communicates with us.

During Bob's class on Exodus, he led us through a meeting place exercise, drawing a connection between our communication with the Holy Spirit and God's heart for social justice liberation.

As I imagined myself meeting with Jesus in one of my favorite places—a high mountain stream in the Cascade Mountains east of my home—I felt like I was striving to *make* something happen. In the midst of this struggle, Bob asked, "Jesus, if there is a place you want to meet other than the one they've chosen, would you take them there now?"

Immediately, I saw myself in an enormous garbage dump, where countless people were sifting through the refuse. Bob continued, "If Jesus took you to a new location, ask, "Why here?"

So I asked, "Why *here,* Jesus?"

I heard, "I want you to *see.*"

This exercise launched me into a journey of *new seeing,* and as I followed the path of my ongoing spiritual liberation, God brought me to this community so that I could begin to *see* how the personal prophetic could be combined with the social justice prophetic in order to proclaim God's heart of *salvation* to the poor and marginalized. In studying the Bible with Bob, I learned that the Greek word *sozo,* which is translated as "to save," also means to rescue, heal, deliver, transform. This expanded understanding of salvation was good news that could make a difference in *this* life—and not just the next. I began to *see* how the good news of Christ's salvation had the power to rescue, heal, liberate, and transform those who had spent so much of their lives standing "with their backs against the wall."[145]

SPEAKING TRUTH TO POWER

As we listen for the heartbeat of God, we will inevitably hear the cries of the excluded and oppressed, the widow and the fatherless, and we will begin to *ache* with God for justice and righteousness (in Greek, these two words are the same). Throughout the Old Testament, and during the time of Jesus, the role of the prophet was to speak the word of the Lord to challenge the political and religious leadership of Israel regarding their oppression of and exclusion of the poor and the outcast.

While prophets called people to repent of personal sin, they were more concerned with *systems* of oppression and exploitation—and they confronted the people who benefitted from those systems. Isaiah gives us an example:

> "Woe to those who make unjust laws, to those who issue oppressive decrees, to deprive the poor of their rights and withhold justice from the oppressed of my people, making widows their prey and robbing the fatherless." (Isa 10:1–2, NIV)

Within the kingdoms of Israel and Judah, prophets such as Isaiah were called by God to speak to and challenge the "anointed" leadership. These prophets were the human embodiment of God's heart, and they intervened in the political and religious affairs of the nation by speaking out about injustices.

At the same time, there were "court prophets" who were part of the ruling administration in the courts of the kings. They are often referred to as "false prophets" in the Old Testament because they only told the kings what they wanted to hear, endorsing their self-serving policies and idolatries, saying "Peace, peace, when there is no peace" (Jer 6:14; 8:11; Ezek 13:10, 16). These court prophets were essentially "yes-men."

But the prophets of Yahweh were political troublemakers, who were rejected and persecuted because "the word of the Lord" that they heard and spoke often challenged the ruling powers, exposing the systems of oppression and criticizing those who benefitted from them. Yahweh's prophets didn't prophesy the party line and were not comfortable in the king's courts. Though we now read these prophetic texts as the inspired word of God and hold them in high regard, we often forget that the prophets were despised and rejected by the mainstream religious and political culture because they challenged the status quo.

The New Testament prophetic tradition begins with the last of the old covenant prophets, John the Baptist, who was arrested and executed for speaking out, and then introduces Jesus, who is *the Prophet*. While Jesus addressed sin and brokenness with compassion, he spoke directly to issues of injustice within Jewish society, challenging the religious leaders for missing God's heart for the people of Israel: "But woe to you Pharisees! For you tithe mint and rue and every herb, and neglect justice and the love of God. These you ought to have done, without neglecting the others" (Luke 11:42).

Jesus directs his prophetic critique at the *religious* leaders of the people of God because they were misrepresenting God's heart through harsh legalism and hypocrisy. Though Jesus doesn't explicitly critique Rome (the political oppressors of his day), his political theology of a new kingdom with a new king clearly threatened the Roman Empire, for the state conspired with the Jewish leaders for Jesus to be executed.

In Mark's Gospel, we learn that after Jesus healed the man with the withered hand on the Sabbath, "the Pharisees went out and immediately held counsel with the Herodians against him, [plotting] how to destroy him" (Mark 3:6). The Pharisees were religious leaders, and the Herodians were secular politicians. In Luke's Gospel, after Herod's soldiers mock and abuse Jesus, we learn that "Herod and Pilate became friends with each other that very day, for before this they had been at enmity with each other" (Luke 23:12).

Jesus' prophetic critique calls us to follow him, warning that we will experience the same fate:

> "Blessed are those who are persecuted for righteousness' [justice'] sake, for theirs is the kingdom of heaven. Blessed are you when others revile you and persecute you and utter all kinds of evil against you falsely on my account. Rejoice and be glad, for so they persecuted the prophets who were before you." (Matt 5:10–12)

This passage is not referring to persecution simply for what we *believe* about Jesus (e.g., Son of God, Savior, etc.), but for prophetically proclaiming a different kingdom and Jesus as the new king that will challenge the values and systems of empires and religious structures, just as the prophets who were before us.

In *Sinners in the Hands of a Loving God*, Brian Zahnd points out that "God's contention with empire is one of the major themes of the Bible. From Egypt and Assyria to Babylon and Rome, the prophets constantly critique empire as a direct challenge to the sovereignty of God. This prophetic tradition of empire critique reaches its apex in the book of Revelation. . . . John wants his readers, who he fears are slipping into a complacent complicity with Rome, to remember that Rome isn't evil only when it persecutes Christians; rather, Rome is *always* evil because of its idolatry and injustice."[146]

WHICH SIDE IS GOD'S SIDE?

Those who seek to proclaim to the church, government, nation, and world what is on God's heart regarding justice must not be tied to any party, as if one particular party represents God's agenda on the earth. For Jesus is not on the side of the religious leaders (Pharisees or Sadducees), nor the politicians (Herodians or Romans), and he does not speak for the right or the left. Rather, Jesus *reveals* God's heart most clearly when he stands in solidarity *with* the poor and the oppressed.

Pastor Rich Villodas guides his church through the desire to pick a side: "The Church is not to be found at the center of a left/right political world. The Church is to be a species of its own kind, confounding left, right, and so-called middle, and finding its identity from the "center" of God's life."[147]

Bob often tells me that one of the greatest dangers of our time is the alignment of prophetic movements with political movements, which then claim that whatever their political side is doing is the embodiment of the kingdom of God. He sees the implementation of some law or agenda as an embodiment of the kingdom as extremely dangerous since the prophetic tradition is neither liberal nor conservative. He emphasizes how "part of the prophetic role today should include critiquing Christian collusion with political powers on both sides."

In the United States, the present political and religious atmosphere leaves no room for critique or disagreement on either side. Evangelical and "prophetic charismatic" Republicans declared that Donald Trump was God's chosen one, who will bring the nation back to its "biblical foundations." Either you back up him and his agenda or you are painted as a godless socialist who hates America. Democrats and progressives often elevate a "wokeness" regarding social justice issues, imposing an equally heavy-handed moralism that "cancels" you if you don't agree with every aspect of their take on all the issues. Neither side leaves room to question or disagree with various parts of either agenda. You must accept it all, or you are thrown out and cancelled.

Yet there is no political party that represents the kingdom of God or speaks the heart of God! Thus there is no pure party, no clean vote. During the 2016 election, one of my conservative "prophetic" friends sent me an article from *Charisma Magazine* that said there was a demonic principality behind the Democratic party. I responded by saying, "Of course there is! But you're kidding yourself if you think there isn't one behind the Republican party, as well."

Brian Zahnd challenges the idea that any political party that could represent Jesus, arguing that "This begs the question of why Christians get so worked up over which side has the most representatives in Congress when the entire system is incapable of implementing what Jesus taught" about non-violence and enemy love.[148]

Bob Ekblad takes up this challenge, encouraging us "to think about things differently than the world and the various cultures and upbringings that have shaped us, and which have given us idolatrous filters. We want to call the Church to come out of Babylon and to bear witness to an alternate reality. We need to think about how we think about issues. Where do our values come from? We need to be informed from above and be informed accurately from below."[149]

There are many prophetic voices in the church that can inform us today. Prophetic voices such as Dr. Jemar Tisby, Kristin Kobes Du Mez, Brian Zahnd, and Shane Claiborne speak about the collusion of the Western church with the vision of the American dream called "Christian Nationalism."[150] Craig Greenfield, New Zealand activist and the founder of "Alongsiders International," a grassroots youth movement working in 21 countries, speaks prophetically about the heart of God for the poor and powerless when he says, "If your Christianity does not plant itself firmly within the camp of the oppressed, your Christianity is in God's way."[151]

African American prophetic voices, such as James Baldwin, Howard Thurman, James Cone, Dr. Jemar Tisby, Dr. Esau McCaulley, Dr. Cornell West, Bryan Stevenson, Brenda Salter-McNeil, Michelle Alexander, Isabel Wilkerson, and many others have expressed the grieving heart of God on behalf of the ongoing African American experience of systemic racism and white-supremacy in law enforcement, sentencing and incarceration, social services, education, employment, housing, and every single aspect of life.

HOW CAN WE RESPOND?

There are so many people in so many places crying out for justice in the world—refugees and immigrants, those trapped in sex trafficking and slavery, those who continue to suffer from racism and white supremacy, homelessness, addictions, and mental illness, those who are caught in the foster care to prison pipeline, those waiting for justice within a biased "justice" system, and so many more. If we want to *hear* God's heart for those who are crying out for justice, we can easily become overwhelmed by all that we are *seeing*.

If we are going to hear the fullness of God's heartbeat, we need to get outside our cultural bubbles by being in relationships with people who are different than us—those who are privileged and poor, on the margins and in the mainstream, people of color and white. Bob notes that the prophet serves "as the frontline witness" to oppression, and he encourages us "to speak directly from what we are actually seeing whenever possible. We need to inform ourselves by being in relationship with those who live in the Struggle."[152]

If our lives have been largely free from oppression, we need to ask the Lord to give us eyes to *see* those who are being oppressed around us. And then we need to pray for God to guide us to *people of peace*,[153] who can accompany us into struggling communities for our mutual liberation.

When we have costly relationships with those who are standing "with their backs against the wall,"[154] we will be able to listen and discern how God is inviting us to *respond* to what we see.

Early on in my time with Tierra Nueva, as God was giving me new eyes to see, I met Ramon, a former Latino gang member. One day he had come for prayer and our gang chaplain invited me to pray with them. Ramon told me about the violence and trauma he had experienced as a child that led him to the streets, and how his best friend had died in his arms in a shooting. He talked about how, while he was in jail, God led him to forgive those who had killed his friend. As I listened to this hurting young man, my heart broke, and my judgments were quickly overcome by compassion. God gave me a new mind about those who were involved in gangs and serving time in jail. Although in our journey together I pastored Ramon in Christian faith, he taught me so much more about following Jesus as he demonstrated a heart that was willing to do the hard work of forgiving those who had wronged him and loving his enemies. Ramon is a *person of peace* who helped me to see.

So while we begin with *seeing*, we also need to discern *what* we are seeing—and how God is inviting us to *respond* to what we are seeing. For *seeing* doesn't necessarily lead to *discerning* how to respond with the heart of God. Moses *saw* the injustice of the Egyptian beating the Hebrew, but he *responded* in a way that was not part of God's intention. Rather than waiting to discern how God was inviting him to *respond*, he lashed out in anger and killed the Egyptian. When we seek God's heart regarding justice issues, we need to *wait* to hear how he is inviting us to *see, judge,* and then *act*.

Amidst all that we see, it can be difficult to discern how to respond, because we can so quickly become overwhelmed. So when I begin to feel immobilized, I have started to pray, "Jesus, what is one thing that is grieving your heart that you want me to see? And how are you inviting me to respond?"

I have discovered that when God shows me one thing from his heart, I do not feel as overwhelmed. And he *never* invites me to respond by being an armchair prophet, weighing in on every issue from my Facebook pulpit in a way that costs me very little. For whenever we hear God's heart for the world and discern how we are being invited to respond, the invitation will likely be very costly, for we are following the way of Jesus, who modeled for us that "there is no greater love than to lay down one's life for one's friends" (John 15:13, NLT).

ACTIVATION

Take a moment to quiet yourself, focusing on your breath. If you feel stirred up or resistant, pay attention to where you feel it in your body. Place your hand there and breathe slowly, inviting the presence of Jesus into that place.

Breath prayer: *Jesus, take me deeper into your heart of justice.*

Meeting Place Exercise (This is also an important exercise to be done in our faith community, so that we are listening to God's heart for mission and justice, and not simply reacting to the latest issue).

After spending several minutes with the breath prayer, invite Jesus to lead you to a place where he wants to meet with you. If you are surprised about this meeting place, ask him, *why here?*

Now invite Jesus to show you something in your community or nation that grieves God's heart.

As you *see* this grief, ask, *Why does it grieve you? How do you want me to respond?*[155] *Is there a person of peace who can accompany me?*

You might conclude this exercise with the following prayer:

Lord, show me how I can move beyond simply reading and talking about this to taking real action that makes a difference to those who are suffering . . . Help me to lay down my clever reasons for resisting Your ways and instead step into the freedom and adventure of obedience.[156]

PART III:

ONWARD

Chapter 13

OBSTACLES TO HEARING GOD'S HEART

Surely the Lord is in this place, and I did not know it.

—Genesis 28:16

I n the book *Sonship*, James Jordan declares that 100 percent of the Father's love is pouring out on us, and then he wonders, *why aren't we experiencing it more?* He goes on to observe how "there are blockages within us that hinder that reality from becoming our life,"[157] for these obstacles prevent us from experiencing the fullness of God's love. Then Jordan suggests that if God's "love itself transforms us,"[158] perhaps "the key to spiritual growth" is—as the author of the letter to the Hebrews puts it—for us to "lay aside every weight and the sin that clings so closely" (Heb 12:1), so that we can make room to receive the constant outpouring of God's love. Just as we all have barriers to *receiving* the fullness of God's love, we also have obstacles within us that prevent us from *hearing* God's heart.

MENTAL OBSTACLES

Our mental obstacles are influenced and shaped by many things, but there are messages that we often repeat to ourselves that hinder our spiritual growth, such as: God *doesn't* speak, or, God doesn't speak to *me*.

These mindsets are shaped early in our lives by our experiences and by the people who have authority in our lives. They influence what we believe, how we live it out, and the fruit we are able to taste and experience. In chapter 4, "Heart Theology," I talked about how *projected lies* and *survival lies*[159] have been reinforced so often that they begin to *feel* true to us, and so they can influence how we live. These deceptive messages are like roots in our mind, which produce the fruit of our beliefs about ourselves, about God, and the world around us.

Projected lies are the messages that were spoken to us by people with authority in our lives, such as, "You're stupid," "You'll never amount to anything," "You're a victim," or "God doesn't speak."

Survival lies are the messages we have come to agree with in order to make sense of our negative experiences, which might include, "I will always be rejected," "Nothing ever works out for me," "I can't trust anyone," or, "God doesn't speak *to me.*"

To help counteract these lies, let's see what the Bible has to say about how our minds can be *transformed* by Scripture.

RENEWING YOUR MIND

In Paul's letter to the Romans, he tells us that we are not transformed by working harder to change, but by having our minds *renewed* by "true and proper worship":

> Therefore, I urge you, brothers and sisters, in view of God's mercy, to offer your bodies as a living sacrifice, holy and pleasing to God—this is your true and proper worship. Do not conform to the pattern of this world but *be transformed by the renewing of your mind.* Then you will be able to test and approve what God's will is—His good, pleasing and perfect will. (Rom 12:1–2, emphasis added)

When our minds are renewed by viewing God's extravagant mercy, we will be transformed, and our lives will bear new fruit. We can renew our minds by offering ourselves fully to God, surrendering all our limited ideas about how God operates and communicates with us. Moreover, Paul says that we are not to be squeezed into the shape of the world, as it has even more limited or skewed ideas about who God is and how God works in the world. Rather, we can renew our minds by meditating on God's promises and the truth of his Word.[160]

MENTAL STRONGHOLDS

In Paul's second letter to the Corinthians, he describes our deeply ingrained mindsets as "strongholds":

> The weapons we fight with are not the weapons of the world. On the contrary, they have divine power to demolish strongholds. We demolish arguments and every pretension that sets itself up against the knowledge of God, and we take captive every thought to make it obedient to Christ. (2 Cor 10:4–5)

A stronghold is any belief, argument, or way of thinking that has a *strong hold* on us—"every deceptive fantasy that opposes God and . . . every attitude that is raised up in defiance of the true knowledge of God" (*The Passion Translation*). These strongholds include all the "barriers" that we have "erected against the truth of God" (*The Message*).

We need to recognize these strongholds and invite the Holy Spirit to search us and to reveal these obstacles in the light of Jesus, who is the Truth. Once we have recognized these false beliefs before Christ, we can invite the Holy Spirit to reveal the truth about God to us. This process may involve confession and repentance from false beliefs, and so we will need accompaniment and prayer from others as we seek to be released from these strongholds.

To give an example from my own story, I have struggled for a long time with a *survival lie* that has often falsely filtered what I believe God is saying to me.

For more than nine years, I have met with several men as part of a recovery group. When we first began to work through our personal areas of recovery,[161] I encountered some projected and survival lies that were impacting my sense of self.

When we were invited to choose the lie that felt strongest, I offered, "I don't have what it takes." After speaking this lie out loud, we were each invited to rate the strength of this belief on a scale from one to ten. This lie felt like a seven to me. Then we were invited to enter God's presence and speak the lie to God. After focusing on Jesus in that quiet space, I sensed that I was entering a kind of throne room, with God the Father sitting on the throne in front of me, Jesus sitting on his right, and the Holy Spirit standing beside me.

After speaking this lie out loud, "I don't have what it takes," I started to laugh. For I quickly realized, "Of course, I don't have what it takes! Only you, God, have what it takes!"

Then I sensed God saying, "The lie isn't, 'You don't have what it takes,' but the belief in your own *self-sufficiency*. I didn't create you to be self-sufficient. I created you to be dependent upon me and others. The enemy has taken this truth and attached shame to it."

"What is the truth?" I asked.

Three Scriptures came to my mind: "I can do all things through Him who strengthens me" (Phil 4:13); "Son, you are always with me and all that is mine is yours" (from the story of the prodigal son in Luke 15:31); "If God did not spare His own Son but gave Him up for us all, how will He not also with Him graciously give us all things" (Rom 8:32).

God had given me three truths to counteract this survival lie about my own self-sufficiency: *I can do all things through him. All that is his is mine. He graciously gives me all things.*

I continue to hold to these biblical truths whenever the lie about my self-sufficiency asserts itself. Over time, these truths are renewing my mind and transforming my life.

Selah

Take a moment to reflect on a false belief that may be hindering you from hearing God's heart. In the activation at the end of this chapter, we will return to this stronghold and bring it into the light of Jesus, inviting the Holy Spirit to give you truths from Scripture that can counteract this projected or survival lie.

THEOLOGICAL OBSTACLES

Your mindset about how God speaks to you (or not) is also connected to the theological tradition or unspoken culture of the church that shaped your faith. Some theological traditions use arguments not so much from Scripture as from a desire to explain a lack of experience, such as, "the Holy Spirit isn't active today," or "God only speaks to us through the Bible."

For example, the lead pastor of the Presbyterian Church that I attended in my twenties used to say that "the Holy Spirit is the silent partner in the Trinity, whose job is to point us to Jesus and help us understand the Bible." Functionally, this made the Trinity into a relationship between the Father, Son, and the Holy *Bible*. Though the Holy Spirit was referenced in prayers, the Holy Spirit didn't seem to *do* much of anything. With Jesus, the church, and the Bible, why would we need anything else?

This theology is known as *cessationism*, which teaches that all spiritual gifts, such as prophecy and healing, *ceased* as soon as books of the Bible were assembled. God had already spoken through Jesus and the Bible, so anything else was suspect.

So I spent my early years of faith trying hard to understand the Bible through my intellect and to live rightly by all my efforts. While I had a vague sense of God communicating with me on a few rare occasions, I was largely deaf to his voice. My prayers felt like leaving messages on a divine voice mail, with no expectation that there would ever be a return call or I could have a real conversation with Jesus. It felt to me, as Paul says in a letter to Timothy, that I walked in "the form of godliness but denied the power therein" (2 Tim 3:5). And sadly, my theology seemed to *quench the Spirit* (1 Thess 5:19).

Jack Deere, a professor at Dallas Theological Seminary, describes his journey away from his *dispensationalist* theological tradition in *Surprised by the Power of the Spirit: Discovering How God Speaks and Heals Today*. Dispensationalism, which emerged in the late-1800s, separates God's activity in the world into seven historical dispensations.[162] Though this understanding of God's work through the Spirit is less restricted than cessationism, Deere's recollections suggest how closely they are intertwined:

This absence of New Testament miracles in my experience didn't bother me, however, because I thought God was the one who initiated the change. I was confident that I could prove by Scripture, by theology, and the witness of church history that God had withdrawn the supernatural gifts of the Holy Spirit. I was also confident that he no longer spoke to us except through his written Word.[163]

After encountering a respected Christian leader who believed in deliverance from evil spirits and healing, Deere took a fresh look at his own scriptural arguments and "discovered that his arguments against miraculous gifts were based more on prejudice and lack of personal experience than on the Bible. As soon as (he) became a seeker instead of a skeptic, the Holy Spirit revealed himself in new and surprising ways."[164]

When the theological structures that shape our beliefs limit our understanding of how God can speak or work in the world, we will close our ears to God's voice, and we will not be expecting the Spirit to communicate with us in any way.

LACK OF EXPECTANCY

All these mental and theological obstacles erode our *expectancy* about whether God communicates with us. Brad Jersak describes expectancy as "genuine trust that God will move (even powerfully), but the word is focused on my openness, welcome, and gratitude to God, specifically as a good Father with good gifts, without demanding a particular outcome (even though I'm free to make specific requests)."[165] This open-handed, open-hearted approach to faith—our belief coupled with expectancy—is an essential doorway that we need to walk through if we are going to see, hear, and receive from God.

But when we don't expect God to speak, we'll miss hearing his still, small voice when it comes to us in the midst of our noisy and distracted lives. While God is certainly not at our beck and call, I spent twenty-one years expecting that God would *not* speak to me, or lead me, or heal me, or deliver me, and so I remained unaware of his abiding presence in my life.

Near the end of that long, dry season, I was leading a high school Bible study on Ephesians. After reading Paul's prayer for his readers, that "having the eyes of [their] hearts enlightened, [they] may know . . . what is the immeasurable greatness of his power toward us who believe" (Eph 1:18, 19), one of the students asked, "Where's the power?"

I didn't have an answer from my theology or my experience, and so I squeaked out, "I don't know. Maybe it's forgiveness. That's pretty powerful."

I had never heard any teaching or had any experiences that would lead me to *expect* God to work in power, and so I could not pass on to this student what I myself had not received.

If we do not genuinely trust that the God who is revealed to us in Jesus through the Scriptures can speak to us today, we will miss out on hearing his voice! While the life of following Jesus is not about chasing experiences, the Bible promises more than we are experiencing – that God is speaking and we can hear. If we want to experientially know the God of love and the power of the Holy Spirit, we need to *expect* God to meet us and speak to us!

EXPERIENTIAL OBSTACLES

Sadly, what many people have experienced has not been the love of God but painful wounding in churches that talk a lot about hearing God's voice and the power of the Holy Spirit. In some churches people can feel pressure to have certain experiences as a litmus test of whether they are a part of those who have the Spirit, while in others people may experience hostility in response to honest questions.

In such church cultures, people might be told that every word that comes from a particular leader or group of leaders is "from the Lord," and any questioning is met with shaming or shunning. These "prophetic" leaders often lack humility and present themselves as infallible, lacking accountability, correction, or repentance when their prophecies from the Lord don't come to pass. These churches appear to emphasize power or performance rather than love—contrary to Paul's admonition in 1 Corinthians 13:2. Rather than building up, encouraging, and comforting (as Paul directs in 1 Cor 14:3), people experience varying degrees of what could be called, spiritual abuse.

Such toxic leadership erects painful obstacles in our hearts, a spiritual PTSD preventing us from being able to be open to hearing God's voice of love and compassion. When we try to distance ourselves from these toxic experiences and painful teachings, we can end up rejecting the truth revealed in Jesus, which is that God longs to be present to us, listen to us, and share his heart with us.

Bob Ekblad describes how he was at a revival meeting when he was eight years old, and the minister began to call out people's sins from the front, declaring publicly that God was revealing these things to him. Bob shrank back, afraid that God would expose him in front of everyone in this way.

Years later, as he sought to hear God's voice and be empowered by the Holy Spirit, Bob recognized that he was carrying a wound and a judgment in his heart. For many years, he had distanced himself from anything related to the Holy Spirit because of his early experiences, and this obstacle was hindering him from having a life-giving relationship with God. Once he forgave those who had wronged him and dropped his judgments against them, he began to receive more of what God wanted to communicate with him.

RELATIONAL OBSTACLES

Obviously, if we do not have a living relationship with God, we are probably not trying to listen to his voice. And yet, God is pursuing us in Christ long before we ever enter into a relationship with him! As John puts it, "This is love; not that we loved God but that He loved us" *first* (1 John 4:10). When God begins to woo us, God is communicating with us—even though we may not realize what is happening.

My wife and I have a friend who has had no church experience or exposure to Christianity in her life, and she once told us about all these unsolicited supernatural encounters she was having, where she was overcome by love, peace, and a profound sense of connectedness to the people around her. She didn't understand what was happening, and this got us to talking about how God can speak to us. Though she had not been seeking God, he was speaking to her heart through these encounters.

OBSTACLES FROM SIN

We can also disqualify ourselves from hearing God if we believe that we must first meet certain conditions. We may believe that God will only speak to us *after* we've gotten our lives sorted out, or *once* we have achieved a particular level of holiness and obedience, or *if* we've prayed and fasted, or *when* we are full of faith. While we are always being invited into greater growth in our life of faith, God pursues us *before* we know Him, when we were still opposed to his ways.

Early on, I was told that my sin *separates* me from God, causing God to turn a deaf ear to me. This idea is based in a few Scriptures, such as: "If I had cherished sin in my heart, the Lord would not have listened" (Ps 66:18), along with, "But your iniquities have separated you from your God; your sins have hidden his face from you, so that he will not hear" (Isa 59:2). Yet the theology built on a few verses ignores the overwhelming narrative throughout the Bible, which is that God *comes close* to sinners. Jesus spent so much time with people who were considered sinners that he was mockingly called a "friend of sinners" (Luke 7:34), a title that has become a badge of honor!

Our sin can certainly become an obstacle, for when we move *toward* sin, we are turning *away* from God and pursuing our own will. Or when we choose not to trust him, that posture can keep us from drawing near to him. Or when our hearts are set on sin, we may ignore what God is saying to us. Though our sin can block us, our sin never blocks the love of God, for God is always pursuing us, speaking to us and calling us back.

The Skagit County jail inmates have helped me understand that their sin is not an obstacle to the love of God or God speaking to them—even in the midst of being incarcerated for criminal behavior that they often have not admitted to fully. During one evening Bible study, a young man shared how much he was hearing from God while he was in jail, since he was praying more and reading his Bible all the time—something he didn't do when he was out on the streets. Another inmate offered, "Maybe that's why you get arrested so much. This is the only place God can get your attention!" Everyone laughed.

No matter what we have done, we will never be disqualified from hearing the voice of Jesus, the Good Shepherd. God loves us as his beloved daughters and sons, and he wants to share what is on his heart with us, and so he will partner with us to break through every obstacle, remove false mindsets, forgive every sin, and heal every wound that is keeping us from receiving his love. Remember, your sin can never separate *God* from *you*!

I've already mentioned my friend who says, "If it sounds too good to be true, it's probably Jesus." This perspective can help open our hearts to receive the *good things that* our beloved *Good* Shepherd wants to say to us.

SPIRITUAL OBSTACLES

Resentment and Bitterness

When our wills are bent toward sin, we can block our hearts from listening to God because we don't *want* to know God's heart. But when we "draw near to God," James promises that "he will draw near to [us]" (Jas 4:8). In drawing near to God, we may need to seek forgiveness for something or forgive someone—and this includes ourselves.

At Tierra Nueva, we always had summer baptisms in the Skagit River. To prepare for these, I would meet with people and walk with them through a version of the "seven steps to freedom in Christ" from Neil Anderson's *The Bondage Breaker*.

One summer, a fellow prayer minister and I sat with a young woman, who had been very active in a local gang and had done a lot of damage to herself and others. As we led her in confessing her sins, she began to speak of things in a very general way, saying, "I hurt a lot of people." Prompted by the Spirit, I said, "It's not important for us to know the details of your sin, but the more detailed you are about what you've done, the more freedom and cleansing you will experience." She agreed and began to confess in greater detail and then asked forgiveness for hurting others, and then she forgave herself and forgave those who had wronged her.

Then I spoke the words of forgiveness and cleansing from 1 John 1:9: "If we confess our sins, he is faithful and just to forgive us our sins and to cleanse us from all unrighteousness." I concluded by telling her that she was forgiven in Jesus' name. At that moment, I felt a rush of electricity run through my body, and she experienced the same sense of God's presence moving through her. This experience of confession and forgiving others ushered her into a new season of deepening her relationship with God.

Fear

When we are afraid of hearing what God might say, or if we are afraid of what we think God might ask us to do, we may pull away, because we don't trust that God is truly good. Or we may be afraid that God will tell us to lay down a relationship, job, or part of our identity because it has become an idol. When we are afraid of hearing from God in these ways, we close our hearts and build a wall to protect ourselves.

During my twenties, I was afraid that if I surrendered to God, he would ask me do something I feared—tell me give everything away and go to Africa or stand up in a restaurant to preach the gospel to strangers. These fears caused me to keep God at a distance for a long time.

Other times, I have set parameters with God, telling him that I will only talk about certain things, but other areas are off limits because I am afraid of what he will ask of me. But when I try to get God to talk to me about certain areas while restricting others, I only hear silence. To keep our lines of communication open, I must confess areas of fear or control in my heart and surrender to his grace, goodness, and love. This may call me to step out in obedience to do what I may be afraid to do.

GOD'S SILENCE

Sometimes God's silence is not about any particular obstacle within us. God may be silent to strengthen our faith so that we will "trust in the Lord with all our hearts and lean not on our own understanding"

(Prov 3:5). Or sometimes, God may be silent so that we will learn to be patient and wait for his timing. In *The Deeply Formed Life*, Rich Villodas suggests that we "befriend silence," for "at the core of silent prayer is the commitment to establish relationship with God based on friendship rather than demands."[166]

After God communicated very clearly that it was time for me to move on from my role at Tierra Nueva, where I'd been for over thirteen years, I entered a long season of silent waiting. Though I had a sense of the big picture about what was next, I did not know any of the details. I often felt tempted to get busy building the next thing, and I sometimes felt anxious that God wouldn't tell me what was next, especially when people started to ask what I would be doing. But I continued to sense God inviting me to sit in Psalm 62:1: "For God alone my soul waits in silence." Waiting on God in a place of silence has continued to be my primary mode of moving forward, for the "flesh gives birth to flesh, but the Spirit gives birth to spirit" (John 3:6).

THE OBSTACLE IS THE WAY

When my friend Zach was working through his recovery journey, he often faced personal challenges, overwhelming fears, and legal obstacles. Part of him wanted to avoid the hard inner work or dealing with the consequences of his past. But whenever he encountered an obstacle, rather than complain and avoid, he would tell me, "The thing in the way *is* the way."

He knew that part of his addiction was to create false comfort in order to avoid challenges, pain, and hard work—to find an easier way, to seek comfort. And so part of his recovery included facing the obstacles and finding the way *through* them, instead of *around* them.

While we may have identified many obstacles that hinder us from hearing God's voice, those obstacles aren't problems that we have to get around or push aside so that we can hear God. Each obstacle is a place to interact with Jesus and hear what he has to say to us. Each obstacle can reveal how God is *already* communicating with us. What is *in* the way *is* the way.

ACTIVATION

Take time to focus your attention on Jesus. As you quiet yourself, thank God for his presence with you.

Breathe in, *Holy Spirit.*

Breathe out, *I welcome your truth.*

As you focus on your breath prayer, invite Jesus to respond to one of the following questions:

What is one thing hindering me from hearing your heart?

Is any false belief blocking me from your love?

Am I holding onto any bitterness or resentment?
Do I need to forgive anyone?

Is there a fear you want to bring into the light of your goodness and love?

Is there an obstacle "in the way" that I can receive as "the way"?

Breathe in, *Holy Spirit.*

Breathe out, *I welcome your truth.*

Chapter 14

Temptations in Hearing God's Heart

And the tempter came and said to him,

"If you are the Son of God, command these stones to become
loaves of bread."

But he answered him, "It is written, 'Man shall not live by
bread alone,

but by every word that comes from the mouth of God.'"

Then the devil took him to the holy city and set him on the pinna-
cle of the temple and said to him, "If you are the Son of God, throw
yourself down, for it is written,

'He will command his angels concerning you,' and, 'On their hands
they will bear you up lest you strike your foot against a stone.'"

Jesus said to him, "Again it is written, 'You shall not put the Lord
Your God to the test.'"

—Matthew 4:1–7

Just as we all have obstacles that can block us from hearing God's heart, we also have temptations that can get us off track. In this chapter, I will explore the foundational temptation of trying to build our identity around our experiences of God. Most (if not all) other temptations spring out of this attempt to construct our identity around how we experience God or which gifts we receive through the Spirit. Yet if we base our sense of value on *how* God communicates with us, or *which* gifts we receive from the Holy Spirit, then any challenges we face, or gifts we don't receive, or times we experience God's silence will seem to expose cracks in our sense of self-worth.

While we can always seek to cultivate a greater awareness of and cooperation with the Spirit's gifts, as when we "fan into flames the gift of God in [us] by the laying on of . . . hands" (2 Tim 1:6), we need to remember that these are not gifts we deserve based on merit or anything we have done, but rather are given to us *freely* from our gracious and loving Creator. Our invitation is simply to receive these gifts with humility and thanksgiving. We might respond as David did when he reflected on his unmerited calling to become king: "Who am I, O Sovereign Lord, and what is my family that You have brought me this far? . . . There is no one like You, and there is no God but You, as we have heard with our own ears" (2 Sam 7:18).

When Jesus was in the wilderness for forty days, he was tempted to turn stones to bread, jump off the temple, and bow down and worship the tempter. Yet each of these *external* temptations springs from a more foundational temptation, which is for Jesus *not* to trust what God has said about his identity.

Prior to these temptations in the wilderness, the Father spoke to Jesus in his baptism, saying, "This is my Beloved Son, with whom I am well pleased" (Matt 3:17). We might rephrase this by saying, "*This* child of mine is so fully loved that he *does not have to do anything* to prove himself to me, his father." At this point in Jesus' life, he hadn't healed anyone, cast out any demons, fasted for forty days, called disciples, taught throngs of people, raised anyone from the dead, or challenged religious leaders. He hadn't *done* anything!

If we look at these first two temptations, we can see how the Accuser attacks Jesus' identity as the "Beloved Son," for the Accuser suggests that God's love is conditional by saying, "*If* you are the Son of God . . . ," then, "prove it! Perform (for something that is already his)! Do something that only the Son of God could do! Turn a stone into bread! Throw yourself off the mountain so angels will have to save you!" These temptations highlight our desire to *do* something to validate our identity. Additionally in the Accuser's temptation, he leaves out an essential word about Jesus' identity: *beloved*. Being unconditionally loved is the foundation of Jesus' identity, and so his response to the Accuser is to stay grounded in the foundational relationship of *love* that he shares with his father: *I trust the words of God, not bread, to sustain me. I trust my father to take care of me; I don't need to test him.*

In the book of Acts, Luke tells the story of Simon the magician, who sought to form his identity around how he *performed* and what he could *do*:

> There was a man named Simon, who had previously practiced magic in the city and amazed the people of Samaria, saying that *he himself was someone great. They all paid attention to him,* from the least to the greatest, saying, *"This man is the power of God that is called Great."* And they paid attention to him because for a long time he had amazed them with his magic. (8:9–11, emphasis added)

Luke describes Simon as someone who built up his identity as "someone great" through the use of magic. Magic is about manipulating the supernatural for the sake of personal power and control. Simon starts out by calling himself, "someone great," but then the people begin to describe him as "the *power of God* that is called Great." As his reputation grows, he gets even more "attention" by "amazing" more and more people.

Whenever we talk about "hearing" from God or exercising the gifts of the Spirit, we can so easily shift from thinking that *God* is speaking to thinking that God is speaking *through us*. When we begin to think that we are great, or that people are amazed by what we are doing, or seeking us so that they can hear what God might be saying, we need to remember that we are only receiving a gift from God. We are, as one pastor put it, "just the donkey Jesus rode in on."

Continuing Luke's account from Acts, we learn that when Philip comes to town, Simon suddenly loses his audience, for people start paying attention to what God is doing through Philip:

> But when they believed Philip as he preached good news about the Kingdom of God and the name of Jesus Christ, they were baptized, both men and women. Even Simon himself believed, and after being baptized he continued with Philip. And seeing signs and miracles performed, he was amazed. (Acts 8:12–13)

Now no one is paying attention to Simon or calling him, "the power of God that is called Great." In fact, "even Simon" starts to pay attention to Philip, and eventually he comes to faith in Jesus and is baptized. He starts hanging around Philip because now he is "amazed" by the signs and great miracles Philip does in the name of Jesus.

As the narrative continues, however, Luke reveals what is happening in Simon's heart:

> Now when the apostles at Jerusalem heard that Samaria had received the word of God, they sent to them Peter and John, who came down and prayed for them that they might receive the Holy Spirit, for He had not yet fallen on any of them, but they had only been baptized in the name of the Lord Jesus. Then they laid their hands on them and they received the Holy Spirit.
>
> Now when Simon saw that the Spirit was given through the laying on of hands, he offered them money, saying, "Give me this power also, so that anyone on whom I lay my hands may receive the Holy Spirit."
>
> But Peter said to him, "May your silver perish with you, because you thought you could obtain the gift of God with money! You have neither part nor lot in this matter, for your heart is not right in this matter. Repent, therefore, of this wickedness of yours, and pray to the Lord that, if possible, the intent of your heart may be forgiven you. For I see that you are in the gall of bitterness and in the bond of iniquity. (Acts 8:14–23)

Luke makes it clear that Simon wants to receive the Holy Spirit so that he can have, "*this power* also." First the attention shifted away from Simon to Philip (and Jesus), and now as it shifts to the apostles, Simon sees an opportunity to return to the spotlight by offering money for the gift so that he can restore his identity as one who is "great" because he can use God's power. Peter rebukes the bitter brokenness in Simon's heart, using the word "iniquity," (the Hebrew root which means *twisting*).

While most of us haven't used dark magic to build a name for ourselves, we can all be tempted to *use* the Holy Spirit to build our identity as someone who hears God's voice or operates in certain giftings. To avoid getting sidetracked like Simon, we need to continually ask ourselves, *What is the root of our identity? Where are we getting our sense of value and worth?*

By reflecting on these questions, we can be alerted and adjust our thinking, for as Archer Torrey, the founder of the Jesus Abbey in South Korea, warns us:

> If you think of the Holy Spirit . . . as a mere influence or power, then your thought will constantly be, "How can I get hold of the Holy Spirit and use it?" But if you think of Him in a biblical way, as a Person of divine majesty and glory, your thought will be, "How can the Holy Spirit *get hold of me and use me*?"[167]

When we seek to use the Holy Spirit to build an identity, our sense of self will only be as good as our latest performance. So, if we are not hearing from God, if we are in a time or season of silence, if we don't have a word for someone who is asking, if we can't perform, we may think God has abandoned us, that he is withholding, that we have done something wrong. Instead, we need to come back to our core identity as beloved sons and daughters of our Father, before we've done anything, even if we have "produced" nothing.

Early in the 2021 film version of Frank Herbert's sci-fi classic, *Dune*, Duke Leto Atreides speaks to his son, Paul, about stepping into a leadership role that his son doesn't want. Duke says: "A great man doesn't seek to lead. He's called to it. And he answers. And *if your answer is no, you'll still be the only thing I ever needed you to be. My son*." When I first watched this movie, I was deeply moved and turned to my friend and whispered loudly, "That's the gospel!"

When we disconnect from knowing that we are *already and always loved* by God, we can quickly forget that everything we hear and receive is an unearned gift, graciously and freely given to us by the God who loves us and longs to partner with us. Only our identity as beloved daughters and sons can set us free from building our identity around our performance. For even if we never hear God speak, or can't perform amazing miracles, and even when our answer is no, we will still be who God wants us to be: his beloved daughters and sons.

THE TEMPTATION TO COMPARE

When we begin to believe that God is speaking to us, we may become aware of places of wounding and brokenness within ourselves. Like Simon the magician, we may be tempted to compare ourselves or our gifts with others, as if the gift we receive and what others think of it determines our value. Paul addresses these issues in his letter to the church in Corinth:

> For the body does not consist of one member but of many. If the foot should say, "Because I am not a hand, I do not belong to the body," that would not make it any less a part of the body. And if the ear should say, "Because I am not an eye, I do not belong to the body," that would not make it any less a part of the body. (1 Cor 12:14–16)

When we look at a gift (or the lack of a gift) and compare ourselves with others, we can be tempted to think that those who are up front, or those who do "Christian ministry," or those who hear words for others are *more* gifted than anyone else. Such comparisons breed envy, which can make us feel excluded and diminished instead of loved and cherished just as we are.

In my early years with Tierra Nueva, the People's Seminary hosted weekend classes. Our Friday evening sessions ended with late-night worship and prayer, when our staff would go around in pairs and pray for people, offering whatever we felt we were hearing from God's heart. I always looked forward to these evenings, because I love partnering with God, and I felt affirmed and valuable whenever I received words from God for others.

One Friday, a guest pastor received very detailed, significant words as he prayed for people. As I tried to pray for others, I kept looking over at the long line of people waiting to receive prayer from him and our team leader, and I found myself feeling jealous. In my jealousy, I felt the temptation to compare and envy the "gift" this pastor had received. I also felt tempted to judge and distance myself from him. Because I was feeling less gifted than this guest, my prayers did not produce much fruit, and this only reinforced my sense of feeling resentful and less-gifted. It took some time the following week for me to process this with our team leader to begin to see what was going on in me.

In Paul's letter to the Corinthians, he also talks about the temptation to feel proud or "better than" others:

> The eye cannot say to the hand, "I have no need of you," nor again the head to the feet, "I have no need of you . . . ." (1 Cor 12:21)

When God speaks to us, we can be tempted to think, "*I* hear from God, and that makes me special." In Corinth, this pride became condescending and exclusionary. Sadly, this kind of pride can lead to a prophetic culture that wounds and excludes people who aren't hearing God in the way that is lifted up.

In speaking of the gifts given to the church in Rome, Paul offers the following correction:

> Everyone among you not to think of [themselves] more highly than [they] ought, but to think with sober judgment, each according to the measure of faith that God has assigned. For as in one body we have many members, and the members do not all have the same function, so we, though many, are one Body in Christ, and individually members one of another. Having gifts that differ according to the grace given to us. . . (Rom 12:3–6a)

THE TEMPTATION TO ADD TO A WORD

When we receive communication from God for ourselves or others, we may not receive the whole message. As Paul tells us, "We know *in part*, and we prophesy *in part*" (1 Cor 13:9, emphasis added).

We may be given a single word or phrase, or we may receive an impression or image, or we may have only a vague sense or feeling. Though we are always invited to ask God for more, we often don't often receive a complete message, and so we can be tempted to *add more*.

This temptation to add to what God is saying is common, and so I try to remember what I heard someone suggest: "When God stops speaking, you should, too."

To give an example from my own story, I was having lunch with a friend who was recovering from an illness, and I offered to pray for him. As I prayed, I felt a familiar electric energy that I have come to recognize as the Holy Spirit telling me that he is doing or communicating something. As I experienced this electric communication, I interpreted it to be a confirmation that my friend would be healed, and so I asked if he felt any different. He said, "No."

In my eagerness to see God move and to be part of God's healing, I told my friend that I believed he would be healed by the end of the day. Even as I said these words, I felt something was not quite right, but I wasn't sure if I was uneasy about stepping out in faith or offering an interpretation that was not from God.

When I checked back with my friend the next day, he had not experienced any healing or improvement, and I realized that I had added my own interpretation because of my eagerness for his healing and my desire to be part of it. Later I was able to talk with him about it and apologize for *adding* to whatever God was doing.

This experience taught me that I need to ask the Holy Spirit about what I am experiencing *before* I speak, and I should never add to what the Spirit is saying.

When we add something to what God is saying or doing, we can misrepresent God, which can negatively impact people's faith. Whether the root is pride, ego, or judgment, this temptation to add to God's revelation comes from the flesh. As Paul's asks in his letter to the Galatians: "Having begun in the Spirit, *are you finishing in the flesh?*" (Gal 3:3). This question has been a helpful reminder when I am praying for others.

THE TEMPTATION TO STRIVE AFTER A WORD

When we pray with a sense of expectation that God will speak to us, we can easily begin to *strive* to hear. Though the Holy Spirit stirs us to *ask, seek,* and *knock,* striving comes from our pride and ego and our need to perform. When we are praying for someone, we might feel impatient about waiting on a word from the Lord. Or we might feel embarrassed to admit, "I'm not hearing anything right now." In the examples I shared from my own story above, striving to hear can block our ability to hear (as when I was resenting the guest pastor), and it can lead us to say something that is not from God (as with my sick friend).

When we strive after a word, we are asking God to give us power so that we won't feel like a failure, or that we have a lesser gift than someone else. The Accuser tempts Jesus to jump off the top of the temple so that people will see God's angels and be amazed and convinced that he is the Son of God (Matt 4:5-7). Similarly, while we may want others to have an experience of God that encourages, comforts, or builds them up, we can strive after this like Simon the magician in order to boost our own egos. I have learned that when I find myself striving for a word, I need to examine the cracks in the foundation of my identity and spend time remembering my baptism and centering myself in the truth that I am God's beloved child—*and that is the only thing God ever needs me to be.*

KNOWING YOUR WEAKNESSES

When the Accuser comes to tempt us, he often begins by asking, *"Did God really say . . . ?"* (Gen 3:1). By asking this question, the enemy *twists* (remember that in Hebrew, this is the root for *iniquity*) the truth about the identity we have been given (in the Genesis narrative, Adam and Eve are already *like God* – Gen 1:26-27) into something that is tied to our performance (as the serpent tells Eve, "For God knows that in the day you eat from it your eyes will be opened, and *you will be like God,* knowing good and evil," Gen 3:5).

Yet Jesus is our forerunner, "who in every respect has been tempted as we are" (Heb 4:15), and "because he himself has suffered when tempted, he is able to help those who are being tempted" (Heb 2:18). The temptations Jesus overcame in the wilderness prepared him for his ministry, for there is no ministry or gift without temptations. Yet Jesus, having resisted and rooted himself in his identity as God's *beloved son*, "returned in the power of the Spirit to Galilee" (Luke 4:14).

As we grow in hearing the heartbeat of God, we need to be aware of the weaknesses in the foundation of our identity as God's beloved child, so that we will "not be outwitted by Satan; for we are not ignorant of his designs" (2 Cor 2:11).

Ignatius Loyola spent time observing his own heart and mind, and he developed rules for *discerning* between the movement of the Holy Spirit and "the enemy of human nature." His Rule 14 offers a helpful instruction for the temptations we have been discussing in this chapter:

> As a captain and chief of the army, pitching his camp, and looking at the forces or defenses of a stronghold, attacks it on the weakest side, in like manner the enemy of human nature, roaming about, looks in turn at all our virtues, theological, cardinal, and moral; and where he finds us weakest and most in need for our eternal salvation, there he attacks us and aims at taking us.[168]

The enemy knows our strengths and weaknesses even better than we do, and his plan is to continue to attack us in our weakest places. Until we strengthen these areas through confession and healing and build them on the foundational truth of God's unconditional love and grace for us, the enemy will continue to tempt us and seek to erode our identity as God's beloved son or daughter.

ACTIVATION

Set aside some time to spend alone listening to God. Find a quiet place and bring a journal with you. When you are ready, begin by focusing on your breath.

Breathe in, *Holy Spirit.*
Breathe out, *I welcome your truth.*

As you breathe, invite the Holy Spirit to reveal a weak area in your identity that needs to be strengthened by God's unconditional love. As you continue to listen, reflect on the following questions from Rob Reimer's *Soul Care* in your journal:

> "Fill in the blank: The issue of my value is dependent on
>
> _____.
>
> What do you feel when you are standing on this faulty foundation?
>
> What do you say to yourself?"[169]
>
> Is this weak area connected with the temptation to compare myself with others?
>
> Is this weakness connected with my ego or pride?
>
> Does this stem from a place of vulnerability or shame?
>
> "Then ask the Holy Spirit for a Scripture to replace each lie."[170]

Breathe out, *Holy Spirit.*

Breathe in, *I welcome your truth.*

Receive the truth God brings and invite the Spirit to root your identity in the love of God.

Fill me afresh, Holy Spirit.

Chapter 15

DEEPENING OUR DESIRE FOR GOD'S HEART

"The more we say Yes to the things He says, the more familiar and precious His voice becomes."[171]

—Pete Greig

A s we near the end of this journey into hearing the heartbeat of God, the invitation is always to go deeper. There is always more depth than we could ever imagine, and so it is important to continue to cultivate space to grow in our asking and listening, seeking and longing, knocking and responding.

ASK, SEEK, KNOCK

Asking

In the Gospels, when Jesus begins telling parables, the disciples ask him what they mean, and they wonder why he is teaching through them. Jesus replies cryptically: "To you has been given the secret of the Kingdom of God but for those outside everything is in parables, so that 'they may indeed see but not perceive and may indeed hear but not understand'" (Mark 4:11–12).

The disciples seem to be distinguished from "those outside" because they have followed Jesus' call, and because they are following him, they are led to *ask* him about the parables. *Asking* seems to be at the forefront of many encounters with Jesus, because he wants to grow in relationship with those who are following him. In fact, Jesus encourages us to "ask, and it will be given to [us]; seek, and [we] will find; knock, and it will be opened to [us]" (Matt 7:7).

To *ask*, we must get in touch with our desires and then we must make them known. Even though our "heavenly Father knows what [we] need before [we] ask him" (Matt 6:8), the subsequent verses in this passage invite us to nurture a conversational relationship with God through prayer (6:9–13). In the Gospel of Mark, Jesus asks the blind man, Bartimaeus, "*What* do you want me to *do* for you?" (10:51, emphasis added). While it seems obvious that Bartimaeus wants to see, he is invited to *name* his longing in the presence of Jesus.

If we do not feel that there is much life in our relationship with God, praying may feel empty and dry, as if we are talking to the ceiling. In such a space, it can be difficult to wait with expectancy when asking has left us waiting in silence, and we may eventually want to stop asking altogether. Yet Jesus invites us to *ask*—and when we don't receive an answer, he encourages us to *seek*.

Seeking

When we *seek*, we make intentional space *to look* for something. Are we going beyond asking and searching for the promises of God? The invitation is to go deeper in conversation with God.

To give an example from my own journey, I have lived through seasons when I have intentionally set aside space to give God my attention, and yet I have still felt disconnected from God. Whenever I notice a deep longing to connect with God, I try to name this in prayer. This is my *asking*. And as I remain with that longing, I am sometimes stirred to read the psalms. This becomes a way of *seeking*.

In praying Psalm 42—"As a deer pants for flowing streams, so pants my soul for you, O God. My soul thirst for God, for the living God," (42:1–2)—I connect with the psalmist's longing for God. In praying Psalm 63—"O God, You are my God; earnestly I seek You; my soul thirsts for You; my flesh faints for You as in a dry and weary land where there is no water" (63:1)—I hear my desperate seeking voiced in the psalmist's prayer.

As the longing of my heart resonates with these psalms, their prayers become my prayer, their seeking becomes my seeking, and their words express the desire of my heart. Over time, I have moved into a more intimate space with God, where I begin to sense his presence and hear his voice anew.

Though we may experience long periods of longing and waiting in silence, the invitation to *seek* God—and not just *ask* God to answer our prayers—requires another level of intentionality from us. It may require taking a retreat, or spending several intentional hours away from distractions, unplugged from media or other forms of consolation. We may need to engage in further reading or establish some regular listening practices. *Seeking* may also involve listening with and learning from others, who can reflect and help reframe the stories we tell ourselves.

Knocking

The invitation to *knock* will often lead us into a place of wrestling with God, where we give voice to our complaints. We see this in the movie *The Apostle*, when Sonny Dewey (played by Robert Duval) screams at God: "I'm gonna yell at You, cause I'm mad at You! Give me a sign or something!"[172] Jesus opens the door for such bold interactions with God in his parable of the friend who comes knocking at midnight (Luke 11:5–8) and the parable of the widow pleading her case before the unjust judge (Luke 18:1–8). In both cases, it is persistent *knocking*—and even badgering—that brings about the desired response. While both the awakened neighbor and the unjust judge are simply desperate for the person who is pestering them to *leave*, Jesus seems to be suggesting that if persistent knocking can get the desired response out of such difficult and resistant people, how much more will our generous Father *reward* those who persistently seek him?

When we are wrestling with God, it can be helpful to have others knocking on our behalf, listening with us and for us. In my own journey, I have groups of people who regularly pray for and with me. We share with one another the things that we are wrestling with, and then we listen to God together around the questions we are asking.

If you are earnestly longing to have a deeper relationship with Jesus, the invitation is to continue to ask, seek, and knock.

EAGERLY DESIRE

Paul encourages us to follow our desire for more of God's heart in his first letter to the Corinthians: "Walk in love and *eagerly desire* the spiritual gifts, especially that you would prophesy" (14:1). Earlier, in teaching on the spiritual gifts, Paul says that the Spirit "apportions to each one individually *as he wills*" (12:11). Then he goes into great detail about the importance of not comparing our gifts with others and not thinking that we are better or worse than anyone else (1 Cor 12:14–30). This teaching seems to suggest that we should be happy with whatever we have been given, for it is a gift. But then Paul encourages us to "earnestly desire the higher gifts" (12:31; see also 14:1, quoted above).

"Eagerly desire" (*zeloute*) literally means "to burn with zeal, to strive after, to set one's heart on."[173] We get the passionate words "zealous" and "zealot" from this Greek root. This suggests that we shouldn't be complacent or apathetic about asking, seeking, and *desiring*. Rather, we should burn with desire!

I regularly desire and ask the Holy Spirit for more—words of knowledge and gifts of healing, greater wisdom to lead, deeper prophetic insight, and clearer discernment, because I long for people to know that God sees and loves them, and I yearn for them to experience God's good kingdom tangibly breaking into their lives.

The Holy Spirit gives us these "higher gifts" to build up of the body of Christ by demonstrating the power and goodness of God "for the common good" (1 Cor 12:7), so that our faith "might not rest in the wisdom of men but in the power of God" (1 Cor 2:5). Our longing for these gifts should not be to have more interesting "God" experiences, but so that we can be carriers of the goodness of God to the people around us. So let us "eagerly desire" to be part of the Jesus movement, which is animated by the power and love of God!

During the season when I was transitioning into a new calling, I eagerly asked Jesus for *more* of the spiritual gifts. As I am in a space of listening to leaders and listening to the Holy Spirit, I have continued to ask God for greater discernment so that I can grow in understanding how the Holy Spirit is moving within myself and others.

Shortly after asking for greater discernment, I was at a going away dinner, and as people were praying for me, someone asked, "I sense the Lord wants to give you the gift of discernment. How do you feel about that?" Before bowing my head to receive prayer for this gift, I explained how I'd just been seeking the Lord for that gift. As I move forward in this new season, I continue to ask, seek, knock, and eagerly desire more.

BE STILL

As we seek to cultivate a heart that is inclined to hear God's voice, we will need to become friends with silence and the humility of waiting. Though we may ask, seek, knock, and eagerly desire more from the Spirit, we may experience silence from God. Yet we are not alone, for as the psalmist writes, "For God alone my soul waits in silence" (Ps 62:1).

In these seasons, our invitation is to trust in God's goodness and love as we wait in stillness, having faith that God is with us, and that, in time, we will receive what we need. As Rich Villodas reminds us in *The Deeply Formed Life*, "It's not a stretch to say that our ability to be silent with someone is largely contingent on our level of intimacy or familiarity with that person."[174] Practicing God's presence through seasons of drought or desolation is not about feeling or hearing God, but acknowledging the reality that God is always with us, will never leave us, and therefore we can trust that God is with us right here and right now—even though we might not sense his presence. We *choose* to rest in the truth that God is for us, and like the father in the parable of the Prodigal Son, he is running down the road to embrace us and to gather us up in his arms so that he can give us "the immeasurable riches of his grace in kindness toward us in Christ Jesus" (Eph 2:7).

Rather than thinking that God's silence means that we've done something wrong, or something is wrong with us, silence invites us to camp in this dry and seemingly desolate place, trusting that we are loved and we are not alone, waiting with our hands open until the Lord moves.

Richard Rohr illustrates the tension of silent waiting with open hands by describing a Zen master's conversation with a young disciple:

> The disciple asks, "Is there anything that I can do to make myself enlightened?"
>
> The master replies, "As little as you can do to make the sun rise in the morning."
>
> Exasperated, the disciple asks, "Then of what use are the spiritual exercises you prescribe?"
>
> "To make sure you are not asleep when the sun begins to rise."[175]

The goal of any spiritual practice is not to achieve some measurable outcome, but to hold an expectant and hopeful space, where we remain present with God, regardless of what we feel or what happens (or not). If we hold this space with expectancy and hope but without demand, if we yearn and yield, we will not be asleep when the sun begins to rise.

CULTIVATING INTIMACY WITH GOD

In *Mansions of the Heart*, Thomas Ashbrook offers the following reflection on Teresa of Avila's "Interior Castle": "(God) loves the real you, *not the person you wish you were.* If you look for His love *there* you will miss it. We can't really know God's love for us until we know the one He loves."[176]

As I have written throughout this book, the invitation to hear the heartbeat of God will lead us deeper into our own hearts. This is intimacy, where the discovery of who we are—beloved and broken, sanctified and sinful—is fully known and deeply loved. It is a place of, perhaps, painful vulnerability and yet, growing trust. In this place of knowing and being known, we can venture more deeply into self-awareness and begin to believe our true identity as God's beloved daughters and sons.

Father, take me deeper in your love.

To cultivate intimacy with God, we also need to cultivate intimacy with others, for our interior and exterior worlds impact one another. As John writes, "No one has ever seen God; but *if we love one another, God lives in us,* and his love is made complete in us" (1 John 4:12, NIV, emphasis added). In other words, we discover the love of God as we love others and as we are loved by them.

Earlier, John challenges us by observing: "*If* we say we have fellowship [intimacy] with God while we walk in darkness, we lie and do not practice the truth. But *if* we walk in the light, as he is in the light, we have fellowship [intimacy] with one another . . . ." (1 John 1:6–7). This Scripture suggests that walking in the light includes bringing our darkness into the light with others. We all need to have a few people with whom we can be transparent about our sin and brokenness, and from whom we can receive the good news that "the blood of Jesus cleanses us from all sin" (1 John 1:7b). These people can tangibly remind us that "God loves the *real you,* not the person you wish you were."[177] When we walk in the light and share this kind of vulnerable intimacy with others, we will also grow in intimacy with God.

SCRIPTURE

In *Working the Angles: The Shape of Pastoral Integrity,* Eugene Peterson reflects on the pastoral vocation, observing, "I don't know of any other profession in which it is quite as easy to fake it as ours."[178] He goes on to talk about how pastors can do all the things the church requires of them (preaching, teaching, administration) and yet be completely disconnected from giving attention to their souls through prayer, deeply reading Scripture, and spiritual direction. This inner work roots and grounds us in the lived reality of our belovedness, and when we neglect it, our "work is no longer given its shape by God."[179] This neglect isn't limited to pastors, for we can all find ourselves going through the motions—even when the motions no longer feed our hearts. When this happens, our lives, hearts, and hearing cease to be shaped by God.

As we grow in listening to God's heart, we need to stay rooted and grounded in the gifts, tools, rhythms, and disciplines God that has already given us so that we can know him, discern his heart, and recognize his voice.

Scripture is the prime witness of our faith, revealing the foundational truths about who God is and how God has been understood throughout history. Rather than engaging Scripture as a flat, dry obligation, we can read it through Jesus, the Living Word, as "alive and active, sharper than a two-edged sword" (Heb 4:12).

In *The Voice of Jesus*, Gordon T. Smith connects our ability to know "the inner witness of the Spirit" (one of our discernment questions) with engaging Scripture. He writes:

> We cannot develop our intuitive capacity to recognize the inner witness [God's voice] unless we are women and men who are immersed in Scripture so that the contours of our hearts and minds are ordered and enabled by the Word . . . the inner witness of the Spirit is the necessary compliment of the Scriptures without which the Bible is but an ancient book. But then it follows that we cannot know the inner witness unless we know the written witness.[180]

PRAYER

Another practice that shapes us as we deepen our hearing is the "inner witness" that comes through prayer. In prayer, we communicate and grow in intimacy with God, giving God our full attention as we both speak and listen. In *The Voice of Jesus*, Gordon Smith observes: "We will not recognize the voice of Jesus unless we establish the pattern of listening to the Spirit in our prayers. We learn to listen in prayer. Then, in time, the whole of our lives will be marked by our capacity to listen."[181] Prayer is the place where we give God the greatest amount of our attention, and is, for this reason, the primary place where we grow in hearing God's voice. Prayer is the place where Jesus continues to extend his invitation: *Tell them that I love them and I want to spend time with them.*

WORSHIP

Worship is not just singing, but about bringing all our love, adoration, gratitude, *and* the fullness of our sinful, broken selves intentionally into the presence of Jesus. Beth Moore, an author and Bible teacher, says that she uses the word "focus" to describe worship, arguing that "anything we do with focus deliberately set on God, is worship. Singing, praying, Bible reading but also walking, sitting, silence, laughing, cooking, feasting, recreating, dancing, ailing, dying—ever Godward, ever grateful."[182]

While it is essential to expand our view of what constitutes worship in this way, I have found that praise and musical worship open a space for me where I "draw near to God and he will draw near to (me)" (Jas 4:8) and there is an exchange of love, giving and receiving, adoring and being adored. Here I sense God's presence in a unique way as I offer my heart in communion with his heart.

We see an intimate image of complete focus on Jesus in Luke's account of the woman, who interrupts Jesus as he is dining with a religious leader, to anoint him with an alabaster jar of perfume (Luke 7:36–50). The woman is identified by Luke as "a sinner" (v. 37), possibly a prostitute. She brings the jar of expensive perfume—possibly a tool of her trade— and starts pouring it on Jesus' feet while kissing them and wiping them with her long hair. As she weeps over the brokenness of her life and her radical acceptance by Jesus, she is being judged by others in the room, and yet she doesn't notice, because she is completely transfixed on Jesus. Upon receiving this woman's radical worship, Jesus compares her to the religious leader, noting that "the one who loves much is forgiven much." (v. 47). In worship, we cultivate intimacy with God, focusing our attention on Jesus, and here we become increasingly familiar with his voice.

SURRENDER

Any life of following Jesus will be marked by surrender, for we are following the one, "Who, though in very nature God, did not consider equality with God something to be held onto, but emptied himself, taking on the form of a servant, and being found in human likeness, humbled himself by becoming obedient to the point of death; even death on a cross" (Phil 2:5–8). Paul notes that just as Jesus *emptied* and *humbled* himself, we are to "have the same mind among [our]selves, which is [ours] in Christ Jesus" (Phil 2:5).

In John's Gospel, Jesus declares that "the Son can do nothing of his own accord, but only what he sees the Father doing" (John 5:19, 30). And Jesus later declares, "I do nothing on my own authority, but speak just as the Father taught me" (John 8:28). Jesus tangibly demonstrates this life of full surrender to the Father when he prays in the Garden of Gethsemane on the eve of his crucifixion, "not my will but yours" (Luke 22:42).

We often *start* a conversation with God by wanting to know God's will so that we can decide whether or not we want to surrender to it. But in Paul's letter to the Romans, he reverses that approach:

> In view of God's mercy, offer [surrender] your bodies as living sacrifices, holy and pleasing to God, which is your spiritual act of worship. Do not be conformed to the pattern of this world, but be transformed by the renewing of your mind, then you will be able to discern what is the will of God, what is good and acceptable and perfect. (Rom 12:1–2)

We surrender *first* as an act of worship so that we can disentangle ourselves from worldly mindsets and our own self-serving wills. To discern God's will, we must cultivate hearts that are willing to say, *yes*, to God *before* we've heard what God has to say. The devotional author and theologian A. W. Tozer notes that "Much of our difficulty as seeking Christians stems from our unwillingness to take God as He is and adjust our lives accordingly. We insist upon trying to modify Him and to bring Him nearer to our image."[183]

I am painfully aware of my own places of resistance and fear, where I fail to trust the goodness of God, where I want God to only tell me what I want to hear. My growth comes as I practice saying, *yes*, to the Holy Spirit as soon as I wake up in the morning. I am building this muscle of trusting surrender. Though I may still lean on my own understanding, and I don't always trust God, this practice of saying, *yes*, to the Holy Spirit is deepening space in my heart so that I am postured to respond when I hear God speak.

PRACTICE

The Activations throughout this book have given you several opportunities to practice listening to God's heart. I invite you to return to these exercises as you continue to ask God questions, read Scripture in the companionship of the Holy Spirit, and journal what comes to the surface. As you practice listening to God through Scripture, invite the Spirit to reveal what God wants you to know about God, yourself, and your neighbor. I also encourage you to find others who want to grow in listening to God's heart so that you can practice together, support one another and discern together.[184]

TAKE RISKS

While it can be exciting to hear God's heart and receive communication from the Holy Spirit, God does not speak to us simply because he wants to be heard. As the prophet Isaiah declares: "My word that goes out from My mouth, it shall not return to Me empty, but it shall accomplish that which I purpose" (Isaiah 55:11). God's speaking is always creative and *performative*, and its purpose is to bring forth life and light. The mission of the Holy Spirit is for the kingdom of God to come on earth as it is in heaven (Matt 6:10).

During my time at Tierra Nueva, each week at the end of our communion liturgy, we would pray that the Holy Spirit would "fill us with the power and love of your endless life, that we may take you to a broken and hungry world." The Spirit fills us with power and love *so that* we can be Jesus' witnesses in the world (Acts 1:8). When we hear God's voice and listen to his heart, we are then *led by the Spirit into* the world.

In *Soul Care*, Rob Reimer writes about growing with God, and he challenges us with the following truth: "Your next level with God lies beyond the boundaries of your current experience. The only way to get there is to *risk more* than you are comfortable with."[185]

As we discussed in chapter 10, "Hearing God's Heart for Others: Partnership and Prophecy," God invites us to partner with Jesus in seeking after his lost sheep, proclaiming his heart of love for them as he delivers them from the rule of darkness and proclaims good news to the poor and release to the captives. This inspiring and beautiful mission of Jesus is *our* mission!

We are surrounded all day by desperate people who do not have anyone listening to God on their behalf. How will they ever know God's heart for them if we aren't listening and willing to take the risk to share all that we hear? If we want to grow in hearing God's heart, we need to risk *doing* his will and humbly *sharing* what he says.

BE FILLED

As I have said previously, before we ever said, *yes*, to God, God has already been pursuing us and speaking to us. And there is always more. As Leanne Payne declares in *Listening Prayer*, "All those in earnest about opening their hearts to see and hear God must *ask for and receive* whatever has been lacking in their initiations into Christ."[186] The more includes what God wants to do in us through the Holy Spirit.

We receive the Holy Spirit when we are born again into new life (John 3:3) and the Father and Son make their home in us (John 14:23). As temples of the Holy Spirit (1 Cor 6:19), the Spirit of God's presence dwells *within us*, speaking, leading, teaching, convicting, and transforming us. This is all the inner working of the Holy Spirit.

After his resurrection, Jesus told the disciples, "Do not leave Jerusalem, but wait for the gift my Father promised, which you have heard me speak about. For John baptized with water, but in a few days, you will be baptized with the Holy Spirit" (Acts 1:4–5, emphasis added). That is the Holy Spirit *upon us* for others. To be "baptized with the Holy Spirit," we simply need to *ask* for the Holy Spirit and *eagerly yearn for* the Holy Spirit to fall *upon us* so that we can be supernaturally empowered to pour God's love onto others.

As Jesus promises in Luke's Gospel, "How much *more* will the heavenly Father give the Holy Spirit to those who *ask* Him!" (Luke 11:13, emphasis added).

ACTIVATION

Plan a place and time to be with God, either alone or with others. As you anticipate this time, invite hunger, hope, and expectancy to rise within you.

When the time arrives, begin by praying and waiting on the Spirit. Pause and give some space after each exhale.

Breathe in, *Holy Spirit.*

Breathe out, *I am thirsty.*

Breathe in, *Holy Spirit.*

Breathe out, *come and fill me.*

Breathe in, *Holy Spirit,*

Breathe out, *flow through me to others.*

Breathe in, *Holy Spirit,*

Breathe out, *I ask for your baptism.*

"Father, for this baptism of your Spirit, one that will continue to well up from within me and flow out through me, I give you thanks in advance."[187]

As with Tierra Nueva's communion liturgy, we now pray, *Holy Spirit, fill us afresh with the power and love of your endless life that we may take you to a hungry and broken world.*

Show us, Holy Spirit, where you want us to go and what you want us to do with your power and love.

Epilogue

HEART HOUSE REVISITED

"The prayer preceding all prayers is,
"May it be the real I who speaks. May it be the real Thou that I
speak to.""

—C. S. Lewis, *Letters to Malcolm: Chiefly on Prayer*

R ecently, I have been reflecting on how Jesus, who was mockingly called the "friend of sinners," spent most of his time with
outcasts, tax collectors, the broken and unclean, and those who
sold themselves or were sold by others. He touched these excluded ones
and let himself be touched by them. He shared table fellowship with
them. He went "out of his way" to cross a lake in a deadly storm so he
could come close to the demoniac, who had been cast out, naked and
chained among the dead.[188]

These images of Jesus befriending those who were rejected and
pushed to the margins have gotten me thinking about all the parts of
myself that I have excluded, cast out, pushed down, chained up, and
tried to manage so that they wouldn't disrupt my life and keep me from
the possibility of *belonging*. I know that my angry, impatient, fearful,
people-pleasing, passive-aggressive, and controlling self will never be
accepted by others. And so how can I ever accept the proud, condescending, judging, self-righteous, prejudiced, weak, rebellious parts of myself
that I am desperately trying to hide?

David Benner's *The Gift of Being Yourself* has been a helpful guide
as I have embarked on the journey of trying to learn to welcome *all* the

broken, wounded, and beloved parts of myself into the wide embrace of God's mercy and grace. Benner writes:

> If I only know my strong, competent self and am never able to embrace my weak or insecure self, I am forced to live a lie. I must pretend that I am strong and competent, not simply that I have strong and competent parts or can be strong and competent under certain circumstances. If I refuse to face my deceitful self, I will live an illusion regarding my own integrity. . . . We must be willing to *welcome* these ignored parts as *full members of the family*, slowly allowing them to be softened and healed by love and *integrated into the whole person we are becoming.*[189]

As I move toward this slow integration, I feel both hope and resistance. Should I really accept the excluded and *sinful* parts of myself? Don't the Scriptures teach us that we should "[crucify] the flesh with its passions and desires" (Gal 5:24) and "put off [our] old self" (Eph 4:22)? Aren't we supposed to "put on the new self, which is being renewed after the image of its creator" (Col 3:10) and so be "transformed into the same image" of Jesus (2 Cor 3:18)? And yet Benner perceives that "Self-transformation is always preceded by self-acceptance. And the self you must accept is the *self you actually and truly are* before your self-improvement projects."[190]

The fearful voice within me worries that Benner is advocating some form of cheap grace, excusing my sin or letting me off the hook from the costly and painful process of "putting to death whatever is earthly in [me]" (Col 3:5). But then Benner continues: "Only after we genuinely know and accept *everything* we find within our self can we begin to develop *discernment* to know *what should be crucified and what should be embraced* as an important part of self."[191]

In sitting with all these unwelcome parts of myself in the presence of Jesus, I have sensed the Spirit inviting me to think of them as marginalized sinners, tax collectors in collusion with Empire, cast out demoniacs, and traitors. For so long, I have walled off these excluded ones and called them "unclean." As I prayerfully named these outcasts in the presence of Jesus, I found myself returning to the deep, subterranean chamber of my Heart House, in the round room carved out of stone. You might remember that this room had many doors, but up to this point, only one has been opened: the door of the room called "Pretend."[192]

As I prayerfully spoken these excluded names, all the doors in the chamber popped open. Staring at all these dark entrances, I have begun to pray, "Jesus, friend of sinners, I know you gladly sit at a table with outcasts, and you put your hands on the unclean, and so I ask you to come and sit here with me. I welcome all these sinful, weak parts of myself to the table of your presence. This is the weak, sinful, enemy self you loved so much you died for. Jesus, Son of the Most High God, this is all my offering. I welcome you to make your home among them."

Selah

While I wait in silence on many mornings, I find myself returning to this deep stone chamber with Jesus, and he continues to invite me to keep welcoming all these parts of myself into his presence for healing and my ongoing transformation.

"FOR GOD ALONE MY SOUL WAITS IN SILENCE" (PS 62:1).

Rather than rushing to make something happen when I sit and wait for God in silence, I remind myself that it took six months for me to enter my Heart House. And then it took me many months to journey down the long stairs to the stone chamber—and several months before the first door opened. In all this waiting, Jesus doesn't seem to be in a rush.

As I journey deeper into intimacy with God, I am learning to be patient as I rest my head on his chest and listen attentively for his heart-beat. As I wait, Jesus welcomes greater depths of my heart into the presence of his love. Over time, I am beginning to see my outcast self as Jesus' friend. At this table of welcome and belonging, I am coming to really know that "God showed his love for [me] in this, that *while [I was] still [a sinner]* Christ died for [me]" (Rom 5:6, emphasis added). And as I welcome more and more of my brokenness into the presence of Jesus, the Spirit is revealing more and more of the breadth, length, height, and depth of God's love for me. This is the Father taking me deeper in his love.

As you pray that for yourself, leaning against Jesus' chest and listening for God's heartbeat, I trust that you will come to apprehend more and more of "the love of Christ that is beyond human knowing":

> May He grant you to be strengthened with power through His Spirit in your inner being, so that Christ may dwell in your heart through faith—that you, being rooted and grounded in [the Father's] love, may have the strength to comprehend with all the saints what is the breadth and length and height and depth, and to *know the love of Christ that (is beyond human knowing)*. . . (Eph 3:16–19) (emphasis added)

ACTIVATION

As part of my morning prayer, I have adapted Father Thomas Keating's "The Welcoming Prayer,"[193] as a doorway into the stone chamber of my heart house, where I look forward to meeting with Jesus.

As I sit in silence, I focus my attention on Jesus, thanking God for his *always with me* presence.

As you pray, take time to breathe slowly between each line.

> *Welcome, welcome, welcome Jesus.*
>
> *I welcome every broken, excluded, weak, and hidden part of myself into your presence, Jesus, because I know you are here for my healing.*
>
> *I surrender all my attempts to acquire power and control, and I trust in your love.*
>
> *I surrender all my attempts to acquire affection, belonging, comfort, and pleasure, and I trust in your love.*
>
> *I surrender all my attempts to acquire validation, approval, esteem, and significance, and I trust in your love.*
>
> *I surrender all my attempts to acquire safety, survival, and security, and I trust in your love.*
>
> *I surrender all my attempts to change, manage or fix any situation, circumstance or person (name them), including myself, including you, God.*
>
> *And I welcome your love, Father, your presence, Jesus, your powerful work within me, Holy Spirit.*

ENDNOTES

1   Throughout the book I will refer to God through the Trinitarian lens of Father, Son, and Holy Spirit. As Jesus came in form as a human man, and talked about God as Father, the pronouns used throughout the book regarding God are masculine in form. I recognize that as people are feeling a new freedom to take a harder look at what they believe and name the pain of their experiences, they are stepping back from a lens that has been colored by a church hierarchy and theology built around white male patriarchy. In this light, a book that refers to the idea of God as Father may be triggering. It can be helpful and expansive to note that the Hebrew word for Spirit is feminine in the Hebrew. This has led some people to refer to Holy Spirit as *she*, though translations still default to the Spirit as *he*. As we explore the heart of God, who Jesus referred to as Father, it is important to be clear that God is not limited to gender. God is not a male or a female. In Genesis 1:26-27 we are told that God created humanity in his image, *male and female*. So, while God is not engendered, not male or female, there is something about women and men together that reveal the image of God. And as God is not limited to gender, God as divine parent is not limited to being *Father*.

2   Email conversation with Bradley Jersak (June 3, 2022).

3   *Healing prayer* is an intentional space with 2-3 others who are there to listen to the person receiving prayer and listen to the Holy Spirit about whatever issue the person is bringing. Here we cooperate with the Holy Spirit to release God's power and love so that the one receiving prayer can grow in freedom from sin, sickness and spiritual oppression and enter more into the glorious freedom God has for his children.

5   This is a Hebrew term found in the Psalms that suggests a musical or pregnant pause, an invitation to stop and listen.

6   See Brad Jersak, *Can You Hear Me? Tuning in to the God Who Speaks* (Abbotsford, BC: Fresh Wind Press, 2003), 148.

CHAPTER TWO

7   www.peoplesseminary.org/about-ctmm.

8   *Worship* is more than singing, it is all of life surrendered to and focused toward God. Most of the time in this book, however, I use the term *worship* as the shortcut to refer to musical praise, thanksgiving, lament and listening. I have found that praise and musical worship takes all my daily life lived toward God,

focuses, and opens a space for me where I "draw near to God and he will draw near to (me)" (Jas 4:8) and there is an exchange of love, giving and receiving, adoring and being adored. Here I sense God's presence in a unique way as I offer my heart in communion with his heart.

9   This will be explored more fully in chapter 6 on Heart Healing and Forgiveness.

10   Ruth Haley Barton, *Sacred Rhythms* (Downers Grove, IL: InterVarsity Press, 2006), 151.

11   Barton, *Sacred Rhythms*, 151.

12   Barton, *Sacred Rhythms*, 151, emphasis mine.

13   Barton, *Sacred Rhythms*, 70.

14   Ruth Haley Barton, *Sacred Rhythms* (Downers Grove, IL, InterVarsity Press, 2006), 70.

15   Psalm 46:10.

16   David G. Benner, *The Gift of Being Yourself* (Downers Grove, IL: IVP Books, 2015), 57.

17   Psalm 46:10.

18   Benner, *Gift of Being Yourself*, 60.

19   *Spiritual direction* is a practice that has been a part of the Christian Church for centuries. In historic communities of faith, a spiritual director was an *anam cara*, or committed soul friend offering spiritual accompaniment, who helped the fellow believer pay attention to his/her soul and to the movements of God in his/her life. In short, a spiritual director is a soul friend, a companion on the way, relying on the Holy Spirit to be the One who directs.

20   R. Thomas Ashbrook, *Mansions of the Heart* (San Francisco: Jossey-Boss, 2009), 157.

21   Benner, *Gift of Being Yourself*, 67, emphasis mine.

22   Romans 5:8, 6, 10.

23   1 Corinthians 13:12.

24   Barton, *Sacred Rhythms*, 12.

25   Barton, *Sacred Rhythms*, 25, emphasis mine.

26   Rich Villodas paraphrase of Father Thomas Keating.

CHAPTER 3

27   John 13:23.

28   A. W. Tozer, *The Pursuit of God* (Camp Hill, PA: Christian Publications, 1982), 13.

ENDNOTES

John 17:3, emphasis mine.

30 Ephesians 1:17.

31 Ephesians 3:19.

32 2 Corinthians 3:17–18.

33 John 1:18.

34 Benner, *Gift of Being Yourself*, 27.

35 Accessed online: https://knowgod.com/en/fourlaws/0?utm_source=4laws&utm
_medium=website&utm_campaign=4laws-visit&utm_content=english&cid=
dp-website-4laws-gds-qq-4lawsref-en-822060579823. For more information,
see Appendix.

36 Ephesians 3:16–17.

37 Matthew 23:27.

38 Rob Reimer, *Soul Care* (Franklin, TN: Carpenter's Son Publishing, 2016), 78.

39 Galatians 1:6–9; 5:2; 5:4.

40 John 6:66–69.

41 2 Corinthians 10:5.

42 Matthew 13:3–9,18–23.

CHAPTER FOUR

43 Alex Proyas, *The Crow* (New York: Dimension Films, 1994), 0:42:28.

44 Rich Villodas, *The Deeply Formed Life* (Colorado Springs: Waterbrook, 2020),
115.

45 Simone Pacot, *Evangelizing the Depths*, (Eugene, OR: Cascade Books, 2018), 1.
Used by permission of Wipf and Stock Publishers, www.wipfandstock.com.

46 Pacot, *Evangelizing the Depths*, 29.

47 Pacot, *Evangelizing the Depths*, 23.

48 Romans 1:18, 24, 26, 28.

For more resources on the "wrath of God," see Brad Jersak, *A More Christlike
God*, esp., "Unwrathing God," and *A More Christlike Word*, esp., "Thus Quoth the
Fathers: God's 'Wrath' as Anthropomorphism," along with Brian Zahnd, *Sinners
in the Hands of a Loving God*, esp. "Closing the Book on Vengeance."

49 Jonathan David Helser and Melissa Helser. "Running Home (Spontaneous),"
The Land I'm Living In, track 2. © 2021 Bethel Music Publishing (ASCAP) /
Quiltmaker Music (ASCAP) (admin by Bethel Music Publishing). All Rights
Reserved. Used by Permission.

50 Michael Dye and Patricia Fancher, *The Genesis Process* (1998/2007).

51 Pacot, *Evangelizing the Depths*, 2.

52 I do not know the original source for this list, but I have adapted the original for this activation.

CHAPTER FIVE

53 See also chapter 3, "Jesus is What God has to Say," in Brian Zahnd, *Sinners in the Hands of a Loving God* (New York: Waterbrook, 2017).

54 From Matt 1:2: "You will call his name Creator Sets Free [Jesus] because he will set his people free from their bad hearts and broken ways" *(First Nations Version: An Indigenous Translation of the New Testament).*

55 Zahnd, *Sinners in the Hands of a Loving God*, 11.

56 Emphasis added.

57 Zahnd, *Sinners in the Hands of a Loving God*, 11.

58 Matthew 11:19; Luke 7:34

59 Zahnd, *Sinners in the Hands of a Loving God*, 11.

CHAPTER SIX

60 Simone Pacot, *Evangelizing the Depths* (Eugene, OR: Cascade Books, 2018), 23. See chapter 4, "Heart Theology."

61 Rich Villodas, *The Deeply Formed Life* (Colorado Springs: WaterBrook Publishing, 2020), 115.

62 John 6:68 (paraphrase).

63 The "Seven Steps to Freedom in Christ" include: Counterfeit spirituality vs. Real, Deception vs. Truth, Bitterness vs. Forgiveness, Rebellion vs. Submission, Pride vs. Humility, Bondage vs. Freedom (sin issues), and Curses vs. Blessings.

64 Matthew 6:12.

65 Romans 5:8.

66 Wm. Paul Young, *The Shack* (Los Angeles, Windblown Media, 2007) p. 224.

67 Lin Button, Healing Prayer School (presentation, Tierra Nueva, Mount Vernon, WA, 2013)

68 Rick Richardson, *Experiencing Healing Prayer: How God Turns Our Hurts to Wholeness* (Downers Grove, IL: InterVarsity Press, 2005), 156.

69 Richardson, *Experiencing Healing Prayer*, 155.

70 Deuteronomy 5:16.

71 Richardson, *Experiencing Healing Prayer*, 158.

72 Richardson, *Experiencing Healing Prayer*, 157.

73 Richardson, *Experiencing Healing Prayer*, 159.

CHAPTER SEVEN

74 See chapter 11, "Discerning God's Heart."

75 Brad Jersak, *Can You Hear Me? Tuning in to the God who Speaks* (Abbotsford, BC: Fresh Wind Press, 2012), 20.

76 Not his real name

77 Jersak, *Can You Hear Me?*, 23.

78 See chapter 9, "Giving God Our Attention," and chapter 15, "Deepening Our Desire for God's Heart."

79 James Martin, *The Jesuit Guide to (Almost) Everything* (New York: Harper Collins Publishers, 2010), 128.

80 Ursula K. LeGuin, *The Left Hand of Darkness* (New York: Ace Books, 1969), 246.

81 Not his real name

82 Ephesians 3:18-19

83 Martin, *Jesuit Guide to (Almost) Everything*, 130.

84 Rich Villodas, May 27, 2022. Instagram. https://www.instagram.com/p/CeEI_mZOD5B/, May 31, 2022.

85 Martin, *Jesuit Guide to (Almost) Everything*, 130.

86 Pete Greig and Dave Robers, *Red Storm Rising: How 24-7 Prayer is Awakening a Generation* (Eastbourne, England: Relevant Books, 2005).

87 Accessed online: Havilah Cunningham, Millenialswithmeaning.com, July 30, 2018.

CHAPTER EIGHT

88 Jordan Seng, *Miracle Work: A Down-to-Earth Guide to Supernatural Ministries* (Downers Grove, IL: InterVarsity Press, 2013), 15.

89 Seng, *Miracle Work*, 15.

90 A. W. Tozer, *The Pursuit of God* (Camp Hill, PA: Christian Publications, 1982), 55.

91 Morris Dirks, *Forming the Leader's Soul* (Portland: Soul Formation, 2013), 116.

92 Rick Richardson, *Experiencing Healing Prayer* (Downers Grove, IL: InterVarsity Press, 2005), 64.

93   Personal conversation, December 15, 2022.

94   Philippians 4:3; Revelation 3:5, 13:18, 20:15, 21:27.

95   A helpful and thorough introduction to this topic is Francis MacNutt's *Deliverance from Evil Spirits: A Practical Manual*.

96   Brad Jersak, *Can You Hear Me? Tuning in to the God Who Speaks* (Abbotsford, BC: Fresh Wind Press, 2003), 144.

97   Dunamis conferences are part of the Holy Spirit ministry of Presbyterian Reformed Ministries International (www.prmi.org)

98   Part of *Healing Rooms Ministries International*

99   Jersak, *Can You Hear Me?*, 129–155.

100   Jersak, *Can You Hear Me?*, 154.

101   Jersak, *Can You Hear Me?*, 155.

CHAPTER NINE

102   James Martin, *The Jesuit Guide to (Almost) Everything* (New York: Harper Collins Publishers, 2010), 151.

103   Kevin Dedmon. *The Ultimate Treasure Hunt: A Guide to Supernatural Evangelism through Supernatural Encounters* (Shippensburg, PA: Destiny Image Publishers, 2007).

104   James Martin, *The Jesuit Guide to (Almost) Everything*, 151.

105   Rich Villodas, Instagram post, December 13, 2021, emphasis added. Accessed online: https://www.instagram.com/p/CXbSuUQO0VD/?utm_source=ig_web_copy_link.

106   Martin, *Jesuit Guide to (Almost) Everything*, 144.

107   See ch. 6, "Revolutionary Hearing: Tuning Our Ears to Divine Intelligence," in Bob Ekblad, *Guerrilla Gospel* (Seattle: CreateSpace Independent Publishing Platform, 2018).

108   "Imaginative Contemplation," *pray-as-you-go*, Jesuits in Britain, May 2022. Accessed online: https://pray-as-you-go.org/article/imaginative-contemplation-exercises.

109   Lorie Martin, *Invited: Simple Prayer Exercises for Solitude and Community* (Abbotsford, BC: Fresh Wind Press, 2011).

110   Ruth Haley Barton, *Sacred Rhythms* (Downers Grove, IL: InterVarsity Press, 2006), 56–61.

111   For more on this, see ch. 11, "Discerning God's Heart."

ENDNOTES

CHAPTER TEN

[112] "All Play" is a reference to the drawing game *Pictionary,* when *all* the "picturists" sketch a word simultaneously to their respective teams at the start of the timer.

[113] Graham Cooke, *Approaching the Heart of Prophecy* (Vacaville, CA: Brilliant Books, 2009), 9.

[114] See 1 Corinthians 12:8.

[115] Cooke, *Approaching the Heart of Prophecy,* 33.

[116] Cooke, *Prophecy & Responsibility* (Vacaville, CA: Brilliant Books, 2009), 13.

[117] Cooke, *Prophecy & Responsibility,* 5.

[118] Cooke, *Prophecy & Responsibility,* 43.

CHAPTER ELEVEN

[119] David Benner, *The Gift of Being Yourself: The Sacred Call to Self-Discovery.* (Downers Grove, IL, IVP, 2004), 69.

[120] See ch. 4, "Heart Theology," and ch. 6, "Heart Healing and Forgiveness."

[121] See ch. 8, "A Heart We Can Only Imagine."

[122] Personal conversation, December 15, 2022.

[123] Chris Walker, "Explore the Four Questions of Discernment," March 27, 2020; November 30, 2021. Accessed online: https://www.prmi.org/four-discernment-tests/

[124] See John 1:18: "No one has ever seen God; the only God, who is at the Father's side, he has made him known."

[125] Rich Villodas, "@richvillodas," Instagram, May 19, 2022. Accessed online: https://www.instagram.com/p/Cdsvz2aOf13/ May 18, 2022.

[126] See, for example, his calling of Levi, a tax collector (Luke 5:27–32).

[127] To give just a few examples, he heals a leper (Luke 5:12–16) and a paralytic (Luke 5:17–26); he forgives a sinful woman (Luke 7:36–50); he delivers a demon-possessed man (Luke 8:26–39).

[128] Henri Nouwen with Michael J. Christensen and Rebecca J. Laird, *Spiritual Direction: Wisdom for the Long Walk of Faith* (New York: Harper Collins, 2006), 20-21.

[129] The DTES is a ten-square block area with the highest level of homelessness and intravenous drug use per capita in North America.

[130] Aaron White, January 2020. Facebook. Accessed online: https://www.facebook.com/aaron.white.56808995

[131] John 10:4 paraphrase

132 Leanne Payne, *Listening Prayer: Learning to Hear God's Voice and Keep a Prayer Journal* (Grand Rapids: Baker Books, 1994), 158.

133 Tim Keller, "@timkellernyc," Instagram, January 2, 2022. Accessed online: https://www.instagram.com/p/CYPwqDHLfdR/

134 Keller, Instagram, Accessed online: March 28, 2021.

135 Leanne Payne, *Listening Prayer: Learning to Hear God's Voice and Keep a Prayer Journal* (Grand Rapids: Baker Books, 1994), 23.

136 Hebrews 2:10

137 Philippians 2:5

138 Revelation 5:6

CHAPTER TWELVE

139 Howard Thurman, *Jesus and the Disinherited* (Boston: Beacon Press, 1976), 1.

140 A short list of Scriptures that highlight God's predisposition for the poor and the oppressed includes Deut 10:18; Psa 82:3, 103:6; Isa 1:17; Jer 22:17; Mal 3:5; Luke 4:18; Jas 1:27.

141 Brain Zahnd, *A Farewell to Mars: An Evangelical Pastor's Journey Toward the Biblical Gospel of Peace* (Colorado Springs: David C. Cook, 2014), 154–55.

142 Mark 10:23.

143 Bob Ekblad, *Guerrilla Gospel: Reading the Bible for Liberation in the Power of the Spirit* (Burlington, WA: The People's Seminary Press, 2018), 59.

144 Howard Thurman, *Jesus and the Disinherited* (Boston: Beacon Press, 1976), 1.

145 Brian Zahnd, *Sinners in the Hands of a Loving God* (New York: Waterbrook, 2017), 156–57.

146 Rich Villodas, Instagram post, February 8, 2023, emphasis added. Accessed online: https://www.instagram.com/p/CoaJKlZOwwJ/

147 Zahnd, *Farewell to Mars*, 108.

148 Bob Ekblad, "Prophetic Discernment & Response: the Politics of God vs. Human," The Peoples Seminary, May 31, 2021.

149 For more on this topic, see Greg Boyd, *Myth of a Christian Nation,* Brian Zahnd, *Postcards from Babylon: The Church in American Exile,* and William Stringfellow, *An Ethic for Christians & Other Aliens in a Strange Land.*

150 Craig Greenfield, "@craigasauros," Instagram post, October 8, 2021. Accessed online: https://www.instagram.com/p/CuygzfEBzNn/.

151 Bob Ekblad, "Prophetic Discernment & Response: the Politics of God vs. Human," The Peoples Seminary, May 31, 2021.

152   Matt 10:11; Luke 10:6.

153   Howard Thurman, *Jesus and the Disinherited*, 1.

154   Adapted from Eden & Brad Jersak, *Rivers From Eden: 40 Days of Intimate Conversation with God* (Abbotsford, BC: Fresh Wind Press, 2004), 85.

155   Lectio 365 app, "Love in Practice" morning devotional, May 27, 2021.

CHAPTER THIRTEEN

156   James Jordan, *Sonship: A Journey Into the Father's Heart,* (Taupo, New Zealand: Tree of Life Media, 2012), 42.

157   James Jordan, *Sonship,* 42.

158   See Michael Dye and Patricia Fancher, *The Genesis Process* (1998/2007), 40–45.

159   To revisit the scriptural promises about how God speaks to us, see ch. 7, "Your Heart Already Hears."

160   For more about the Genesis Process, see Michael Dye, *The Genesis Process for Change Groups* (2012).

161   The number of dispensations vary typically from three to eight. Following is a typical seven-dispensation scheme: *1) Innocence:* From Adam prior to the Fall of Man; ends with expulsion from the Garden of Eden. *2) Conscience:* From the Fall to the Great Flood. *3) Human Government:* After the Great Flood, humanity is responsible to enact the death penalty; ends with the dispersion at the Tower of Babel. *4) Promise:* From Abraham to Moses; ends with the refusal to enter Canaan and the forty years of unbelief in the wilderness. *5) Law:* From Moses to the crucifixion of Jesus Christ; ends with the scattering of Israel in AD 70. *6) Grace:* From the cross to the rapture of the church, which is seen by some groups in 1 Thessalonians and Revelation. The rapture is followed by the wrath of God, constituting the Great Tribulation. *7) Millennial Kingdom:* A thousand-year reign of Christ on earth (Rev 20:1–6), centered in Jerusalem, ending with God's judgment on the final rebellion.

162   Jack Deere, *Surprised by the Power of the Holy Spirit* (Grand Rapids: Zondervan, 1993), 14.

163   Jack Deere, *Surprised by the Power of the Holy Spirit,* back cover.

164   Email conversation with Bradley Jersak, June 3, 2022.

165   Rich Villodas, *The Deeply Formed Life* (Waterbrook, 2020), 22–23.

CHAPTER FOURTEEN

166   R. A. Torrey, *The Person and Work of the Holy Spirit,* (Grand Rapids: Zondervan, 1910, 1974), 4.

167   Timothy M. Gallagher, *The Discernment of Spirits: An Ignatian Guide for Everyday Living* (New York: Crossroad Publishing Company, 2005), 174.

168   Dr. Rob Reimer, *Soul Care: 7 Transformational Principles for a Healthy Soul,* (Franklin, TN, Carpenter's Son Publishing, 2016) 71.

169   Dr. Rob Reimer, *Soul Care,* 71.

CHAPTER FIFTEEN

170   Pete Greig, *How to Hear God: A Simple Guide for Normal People* (Grand Rapids: Zondervan, 2022), 235.

171   Robert Duvall, *The Apostle* (1997). Accessed online: https://www.youtube.com/watch?v=q5v5DOEF45E.

172   Thayer's Definition, accessed online: https://www.studylight.org/lexicons/eng/greek/2206.html

173   Rich Villodas, *The Deeply Formed Life: Five Transformative Values to Root Us in the Way of Jesus* (Colorado Springs: Waterbrook, 2020), 23.

174   Richard Rohr, *Everything Belongs: The Gift of Contemplative Prayer* (New York: Crossroad, 2003), 60.

175   R. Thomas Ashbrook, *Mansions of the Heart: Exploring the Seven Stages of Spiritual Growth* (San Francisco: Jossey-Boss, 2009), 157, emphasis added.

176   Ashbrook, *Mansions of the Heart,* 157.

177   Eugene Peterson, *Working the Angles: The Shape of Pastoral Integrity* (Grand Rapids: Eerdmans, 1987), 6

178   Peterson, *Working the Angles,* 5.

179   Gordon T. Smith, *The Voice of Jesus* (Downers Grove: InterVarsity, 2003), 31.

180   Smith, *Voice of Jesus,* 26.

181   Beth Moore, Instagram post (October 9, 2021). Accessed online: https://www.instagram.com/bethmoorelpm

182   A. W. Tozer, *The Pursuit of God* (Camp Hill, PA: Christian Publications, 1982), 101.

183   For resources that can help facilitate these groups, see Eden and Brad Jersak, *Rivers From Eden: 40 Days of Intimate Conversation with God* (Abbotsford, BC: Fresh Wind Press, 2004); Lorie Martin, *Invited: Simple Prayer Exercises for Solitude and Community* (Abbotsford, BC: Fresh Wind Press, 2010).

184   Rob Reimer, *Soul Care: 7 Transformational Principles for a Healthy Soul* (Franklin, TN: Carpenter's Son, 2016), 204.

185   Leanne Payne, *Listening Prayer: Learning to Hear God's Voice and Keep a Prayer Journal* (Grand Rapids: Hamewith, 1994), 144, emphasis added.

ENDNOTES

186   Payne, *Listening Prayer*, 236-237.

EPILOGUE

187   Mark 4:35-5:20

188   David G. Benner, *The Gift of Being Yourself: The Sacred Call to Self-Discovery* (Downers Grove, IL: InterVarsity, 2015), 50–51, emphasis added.

189   Benner, *Gift of Being Yourself*, 53, emphasis added.

190   Benner, *Gift of Being Yourself*, 54–55, emphasis added.

191   See ch. 2, "Invitation to Intimacy."

192   Josefina U. Fernandez, "Practicing the Welcoming Prayer" (October 14, 2016). Accessed online: http://www.prayingfromtheheart.org/?m=201610

Made in United States
Orlando, FL
22 May 2023